Educating All Children

Is It Possible?

David Austin Ph.D

Order this book online at www.trafford.com
or email orders@trafford.com

Most Trafford titles are also available at major online book retailers.

Printed in Victoria, BC, Canada.

ISBN: 978-1-4269-1204-7 (sc)

ISBN: 978-1-4269-1205-4 (dj)

ISBN: 978-1-4269-1206-1 (e-book)

*Our mission is to efficiently provide the world's finest, most comprehensive book publishing
service, enabling every author to experience success. To find out how to publish your book, your
way, and have it available worldwide, visit us online at www.trafford.com*

Trafford rev. 12/16/2009

 www.trafford.com

North America & international
toll-free: 1 888 232 4444 (USA & Canada)
phone: 250 383 6864 ♦ fax: 812 355 4082

To my father, Lewellyn T. Austin, who ensured that his son had a great education, for which I am eternally grateful.

Contents

Foreword

I met Ronnie when I was a doctoral student at Temple University in Philadelphia in 1968. Temple sat in the middle of a large black ghetto in the northern part of the city. My wife ran the women's dormitory and we lived in an apartment on the first floor. The building faced the main road, aptly named Broad Street, and was surrounded by an iron fence. At the main entrance, through which everyone had to pass, some of the neighborhood kids would hang out hoping that the students would pay them to clean their shoes. The boys used to make a big fuss of my daughter Candace, who was four at the time. Ronnie was a particular friend and gradually I came to know his story.

He lived in the neighborhood with his mother and brothers and sisters. The father had died under somewhat mysterious circumstance following a card game. The family was on welfare. One brother had already been in jail, and a sister had a baby but no husband. Ronnie was about 14 and went to the local public school. Schools in Philadelphia at that time were quite awful and Ronnie was not learning much. However he was well-behaved, so was promoted every year. The other boys called him Oreo, a cookie which is black on the outside but white on the inside. There was not enough to eat at home, and Ronnie was sometimes reduced to eating starch to allay his hunger. There were not enough beds, and as one of the younger children he had to sleep on the couch in the living room, competing with the color television.

My wife and I decided to do something about him.

The first thing we did was to pay him for getting good grades in school. This had an immediate and positive effect. The second thing we did was to feed him by the simple expedient of giving him access to the dorm's cafeteria. The third thing we did was to make him a part of the family by hiring him to babysit. It was not that his mother did not love him or care about him, but she did not have the resources to do anything about it.

Ronnie became a success. He graduated from high school, went to junior college, was accepted into the Pennsylvania State Police Academy, married – a white girl - had two daughters, and achieved a life. Forty years later he is retired, still married to the same girl, and lives in his own house in the suburbs.

Compare him to me. I grew up in England and received, arguably, the best education it was possible to have, simply because I happened to be born to a father who wanted the best for his children, and had the resources to give them that. I started off in a village school in Nelson, Wales but at age ten my father enrolled me in a private preparatory boarding school. At age thirteen I went to a private elite boarding school. After military service I went on to Cambridge University, and took a degree in law. I lived a very pleasant life and had a childhood which I remember with fondness and respect. I was never hungry, it never crossed my mind that I was not loved, I thought drugs were something that doctors prescribed, I enjoyed my various schools, and I did not know what poverty was.

Life is not fair. So much depends on the lottery of birth. Education is an immense and very expensive effort to level the playing field. Currently in both England and America more children stay in school and more go on to college, but certain groups do much better in the aggregate than others. It is for this reason that it is almost impossible to find a book that has anything good to say about education in either country. In both countries the best schools and the best students are as good as any in the world. Where both countries fail is in their attempt to make sure that all children are well educated no matter their parents' income, no matter the color of their skin. The question is, why?

I will look first at students, and what they bring to their education. I will then look at parents, teachers, schools, the bureaucracy, and life beyond high school. Finally I will look at why we do not seem to know what to do, and offer my own suggestions.

Chapter One

What Do Students Bring To School?

Schools are defined by their students, specifically by how their students do on the various exams they have to take. Students do not come to school as blank slates. No matter at what age they start formal schooling, and no matter which school they attend, they bring with them a lot of baggage, some of it positive and some of it negative. Let me summarize that baggage.

Genetic Endowment

"Differences in the amount of gray matter in the frontal lobes are not only genetically influenced but are significantly correlated with differences in intelligence." Steven Pinker.

"Genes account for none of the difference in IQ between blacks and whites; measurable environmental factors plausibly account for all of it." Richard Nisbett

In 2009 Chris Woodhead in England made a stir by claiming that middle class children had better genes than lower class children. His words were widely reported because he was a former chief schools inspector, and currently an education professor. Predictably some academics berated him and some academics supported him.

A lot of ink has been spent in both America and England discussing whether certain groups differ as groups in their genetic endowment, especially in regard to intelligence. I shall have more to say about this later. It is a fact however that individuals do differ genetically across a whole host of factors, and one of these factors is intelligence, however defined. I think Howard Gardner is correct when he argues that there is more than one kind of intelligence, and if so this must surely be the result of genetics. I had a friend who was a professor of physics at Aston University in England. He said that physicists thought differently than people who were not physicists, and I believed him. I could not understand a word he said! Some people are simply brighter than other people, some people have talents that other people do not have. The important point to remember, however, is that intellectual development, however defined, is not 100% genetically constrained. Education cannot change genes, and needs to focus on what it can change, which is the component of development which is not genetic, whether it be 20%, 35%, or 50%. Moreover the fact that genes may account for all kinds of differences, does not mean that there is a genetic explanation for any difference that is found between groups. If there were, then it would seem that Finns, who do well on international education tests, are genetically superior to both Americans and Englishmen.

In order to try and make myself clear I want to introduce a new word, acintel. Acintel refers to the ability to do well in school, and is short for academic intelligence. It is what schools measure when they give students tests. It is what countries measure when they give standardized exams. It is what gets you into the college of your choice, and into the career of your choice. To my knowledge I have never taken an intelligence test, so I have no idea what my IQ is, but I have a clear idea what my acintel is, and that is what has been important. Clearly it helps to be born intelligent, whatever that means, but that is only one component of acintel.

To be admitted to most colleges in America it is necessary to take one of two national tests, labeled ACT and SAT. Both tests produce scores on the core subjects. Both tests are given nationally, so that their results can be used to compare individuals against the group, and groups against each other. ACT produces a composite score with a high of 36. It is based on the results of test components in English, Math, and Science. Anyone scoring 36, which means that they are better than 99% of other students who have taken the test, will not only gain easy admission to the college of their choice, but will be awarded a significant amount of scholarship money. If on the other hand you obtain a score of 18 your chances of getting into Harvard are nil, although there will still be plenty of lesser colleges who will accept you. In England students take subject exams and the more subjects they score well in, the more likely they are to be accepted to the college of their choice. The two systems are similar – they are methods for sorting out who goes where. To get into a good university, therefore, it is necessary to learn to do well on these tests, and to a large extent, that is what education is all about.

To obtain a high score on these exams certainly requires intelligence, but it also requires a high level of acintel, and this can be taught. There is a whole industry in both countries geared towards training students to excel on these tests, and the most important industry is of course the educational system. No matter how intelligent you are, it helps if you have attended a good school and have been well educated. At the private schools I attended in England, Chelmsford Hall and Tonbridge, the boys – there were no girls – all came from a narrow band of academic competence. They were all relatively at the same level. Their fathers had paid high fees, and expected the schools to deliver. The schools in turn had to deliver, or take the risk of losing admissions. The job of Chelmsford Hall, which admitted boys from age 6 to 12, was to have boys accepted by one of England's elite boarding schools. The job of Tonbridge, which admitted boys at age 12 or 13, was to have boys accepted into an elite university, preferably Oxford or Cambridge. Both schools were successful at doing this. There is an identical system in America. Both systems are excellent at what they do.

Private schools are, of course, selective. They select partly by having high fees, partly by how students perform on exams, partly through interviews, and partly by looking at how the student has performed in his previous educational settings. By comparison, public state schools – throughout this book I will call schools funded with public monies public, as opposed to schools which are funded through fees which I will call private - with certain exceptions, have to take whoever lives in their catchment area. The result of course is that while a teacher in a private school is faced with a relatively small group of students who are well behaved, high in acintel, and want to learn, the teacher in a public school is faced with students whose acintel is all over the place, some of whom do not want to be there, some of whom have no respect for the school or its teachers. For that reason a teacher in a public school has a far harder task than a teacher in a private school, especially if the school is in an inner city setting with students who are not only poor but from vastly different backgrounds and often nowadays with different languages.

My own children have been to a number of different schools. Some of them have been private and similar to Chelmsford Hall. When I was living in Philadephia at Temple there was no way I would have sent my children to the local public schools, so I did the same thing as President Obama and other Presidents have done who are forced to live in Washington D.C., I sent them to a private school. When I lived in pleasant suburbs, I sent them to the local public school. The students were still selected, in the sense that they came from a relatively homogeneous residential setting. In Bethlehem, for instance, the students were a mixed bunch because there were both upper and lower class residential areas in the catchment area. The school solved the problem to some extent by tracking the students into different levels within a subject, so that there were multiple classes in math and the better students were placed in one class, and the poorer students in another. But it did not solve all problems. I remember talking with one of the brighter students. She said one of her frustrations was that at the beginning of each academic year the teacher would have to go over the material which had been taught the previous year, but which most of the students had forgotten over the summer. She said that she sat at the back of the class and did crossword puzzles and 'rejoined' the class when everyone else had caught up. I shall return to the problem of lengthy summer vacations again later on.

School is difficult for a student if they have not been adequately prepared. Education is cumulative, so that if a student does not learn Algebra One properly, he is obviously going to have a problem with Algebra Two. If he has not learned to read fluently in primary school, he is obviously going to have a problem studying Literature in High

School. My own first school was a public school in Nelson, Wales, my father's hometown, which I attended from age 6 to 10. I went there because of the war. My father worked and lived in London, and the government urged parents to send their children to the countryside because of a fear of bombing raids. My father realized that the school in Nelson was inadequate, so at age 10 I went to Chelmsford Hall. I have a letter written by the Headmaster of Chelmsford Hall to Tonbridge on the occasion of my application for admission. In it he writes: "David came rather late to this school, having previously attended a school in Wales where he had no chance of starting Latin, Algebra, and Geometry." Needless to say, Chelmsford Hall succeeded in bringing me up to standard by the time I applied to Tonbridge three years later. Had I stayed in Wales, this would not have happened, and the whole trajectory of my life would have been different!

When I first came to America I was hired by the College of New Jersey to develop and direct an Upward Bound program. The intent of this program, which was a national program funded by the federal government and part of Johnson's War on Poverty, was to identify students in high school who were not performing at their potential, to bring them on a college campus for a summer program, and thereby hopefully to motivate them to aspire and plan to go to college. The first problem we had was in convincing the schools that we did not want their best students. The second problem was in developing a summer program of relatively short duration which would succeed in motivating the students. The third problem was that these were high school students. We had a great time. The students had a great time. Whether or not we were successful in achieving our goal was not so clear and certainly not measured. I suspect that many of the students had significant academic deficiencies which were not touched.

More recently my younger children attended a school in the hill country in Texas, in the middle of nowhere. It was a small school, with less than 300 students from kindergarten through 12th grade. Classes were small. Many of the students were Hispanic, their families coming originally from Mexico. Many of them were poor, their families, when they had them, surviving on welfare. As in every school, there were some bright students and some dull students, and some in between. Most of the students had no plans to go to college. One of the students,

Jamie, sticks in my mind. He knew what he wanted to do, he was highly motivated, he did well on the ACT, and he was accepted at M.I.T. one of the most prestigious universities in America. It helped that his father were very supportive. As his mother told me, if they had to mortgage the ranch to get their son where he wanted to be, they would. Another boy, also bright, good at English, aspired to be a journalist. His father was Hispanic and worked as a laborer with the local township. The family had little money. The boy was hoping to go to a community college in San Antonio.

These were the good students. There were plenty of poor students. At least one high school girl got pregnant each year the six years we were there. Many of the students seemed to have no plan for their lives. A number went into the military, and this was a good option, as it is for all lower class kids for whom college does not seem a realistic choice. When we first moved there I was friendly with one of the graduating seniors who was going to college to study to be a teacher. I asked her what another student, who ranked third in the class, was planning to do. I assumed she also would be going to college. Oh no, I was told, she has to buy a truck.

At another point in my life I was Deputy Superintendent of a Children's Home near London called Hutton Poplars. It served 300 children from birth to 18. Some of the children were there because they had got into trouble with the law, but others were simply in need of care, having no one who could look after them. Leslie was one of these children. He was about 14 and came from the East End (the poor part) of London. He spoke like an East Ender, and had a working class face, old before its time. His background was appalling. But the remarkable thing about Leslie was that not only did he like classical music, but he was also a very talented artist. On the wall of my study hangs a self-portrait done in oil which could easily be taken as a Van Gogh. Nothing in his background would have predicted this. Talents come out of nowhere, from the genes you are born with. What Leslie might have achieved had he enjoyed a supported life, I do not know. As it was his grades at school were nowhere near enough to allow him to go to college, even if he could have afforded to do so. The superintendent wanted to apprentice him to a butcher, but my wife and I decided to try and get him some formal training in art. He did not have the self-discipline for this and dropped out. My wife and I left for America shortly afterwards but we continued to correspond. Leslie ended up working in sales, married, had children, acquired a council flat, and managed to achieve a stable life. I like to think that we were of some help.

The main issue with genes is what, given that they cannot be changed, can be done to either enhance their effects if they are positive, or adjust for their effects if they are negative. I spent a large part of my life running programs for people with autism and mental retardation and other similar disabilities. They were very impaired, many of them with identifiable organic, chromosomal, or chemical problems. None of them suddenly or even gradually became normal. They all had IQs below 70 and represent about 2% of the population. Some of them had medically identifiable problems, but in many cases there was no known cause for their condition, it was simply assumed that at some point, possibly during the birthing process, their brains had been damaged. On the other hand many children score low on IQ tests not because their brains are damaged or because they have chromosomal anomalies, but because they have had impoverished lives. For three years I worked with street kids in Naples, Italy. As far as I could tell their brains functioned perfectly well. They had no problem dealing with the specific challenges of their lives – living on the streets requires a high degree of street savvy – but they totally lacked the kinds of academic skills which are so valued in our developed societies, and the lack of which restricts many opportunities. With rare exceptions they ended up as common laborers or, at best, factory workers.

Clearly any educational system should aspire to support students achieving their highest potential, whatever that is, and all educational systems have to believe that children can learn unless it can be documented beyond doubt that for a clearly identified reason they cannot. Too often this is not done. Recently I was meeting with the headmaster of a local school, and he seemed to believe that students came to school with certain characteristic behaviors, and that there was nothing the school could do about this. This is surely incorrect, but too often this is what happens.

Money

"Money is like a sixth sense without which you cannot make a complete use of the other five." Somerset Maugham

"The poor always ye have with you." St. John.

"Unto everyone that hath shall be given, and he shall have abundance: but from him that hath not shall be taken away even that which he hath." St. Matthew.

At Chelmsford Hall and Tonbridge the students came from the same or very similar socio-economic category of society for the simple reason that their parents had to be able to pay the fees which at Tonbridge now amount to $40,000 a year. Everyone wore the school uniform, no one had cars, everyone ate the same food, and were housed in similar settings if they were boarders. They all spoke with the same accent, they were all white, and they all belonged to the Church of England. And they all had money. In public schools the situation is very different, especially in the United States, and increasingly so in England.

When I came to the United States in 1965 I was ecstatic about Johnson's War on Poverty. Here was the richest nation on earth ready to do away with poverty. Alas, while there was some success, overall the program was a failure. The Vietnam war, among other things, sucked the blood right out of it. Medicare certainly helped the elderly, and remains a very popular program, and Medicaid provided necessary medical access to poor people, but neither program did anything about poverty itself. Poverty, in both England and America, has proved to be an intractable problem. Politicians are always stating what they are going to do about it, and somehow poverty just goes marching on. Recently there have been reports that childhood poverty has been increasing in both countries, which is frightening. Both countries spend enormous sums on welfare programs of various kinds which seem too often to simply perpetuate poverty rather than remove it. In both countries there are families where three generations have all been on welfare. It appears to be addictive.

Children without money live very different lives from children with money, across multiple dimensions, and this is very difficult for people with money to understand. This was very apparent in Texas. While family breakdown is not unique to the poor, its negative effects are more dramatic. When rich people break up they simply sit down with their lawyers and divide the loot, sometimes peacefully and sometimes not. In either case provision is made for the welfare of the children, who typically end up with mother. Many of the students in Texas were not only poor, but endured very chaotic lives, and families broke up without any agreement as to what to do with the children. In Texas so many children were coming to school without having had breakfast, even children with families, that the State started providing this at school, to all students. My wife worked for a while with an elementary school student who had significant behavioral problems which interfered with his academic performance, even though he was very bright. His mother cared about him, but she had multiple children by more than one father, so that the home situation was unstable. Needless to say the student was put on medication, which has become the automatic response to many problems, but this did not resolve the situation. Towards the end of our stay his mother found a good man and married him. Even though the man had been married and had children of his own, he brought stability to the situation. The student's behavior immediately improved which of course allowed him to do better academically.

Poverty is related to academic performance, so that schools which are located in poor areas do less well on the various exams than schools which are located in rich areas. The rich can enhance their child's education in various ways. In 2004 the University of London's Institute of Education reported that 27% of the students across all grades in public schools received private tutoring paid for by their parents. Obviously children of parents who can afford to do this have an advantage. Equally obviously it means that the parents are very interested in their children's education. When I was at Tonbridge my language master used to organize group tours to Europe. My first visits to Venice, Vienna, and Paris were all done with him, and they all cost money. Ronnie when we met him had never been out of Philadelphia, and had never been on a train.

In England in 2008 one in five children, amounting to 2.2 million, are growing up in households which are entirely funded through benefits. Britain has the highest percentage in Europe of such children. This is despite the fact that the Labor Party which has been in power for the past 12 years has been committed to eradicating poverty. Another report in 2007 claimed that poor children are no more likely to escape the poverty trap than they were 30 years ago. It went on to state that by age seven bright children from poverty backgrounds are overtaken at school by less gifted students from wealthy families. In another 2008 report 21% of poor children obtained five A to C grades including maths and English, as opposed to 49% of children who were not poor. Furthermore it found that this gap increases as the children progress through school. Poor children were also more likely to be persistent truants, more likely to be suspended for aggressive behavior, and more likely to quit school.

The situation is similar in America.

Given that some people are always going to be richer than others and can give their children benefits which are not available to poor children, I cannot see this changing. If poor children are to have the same stimulating and enriching experiences as rich children then this has to be planned for and paid for. That is easier said than done. I remember reading an article by a student who attends Colorado College in America on a scholarship. She said that while the scholarship paid her fees she still had to sit in her dorm room while the other students went off skiing!

This process has to start early. How do you arrange things so that poor parents help their children with homework, buy them books, send them on trips, and purchase tutoring? I think that if one could eradicate poverty, that would take care of most educational problems. Middle class parents raise their children to value education, poor parents do not, so the solution is obviously to make everyone middle class. Much easier said than done. I shall have more to say about this later.

Race, Ethnicity, and Religion

"I want to be the white man's brother, not his brother-in-law".
Martin Luther King.

When I grew up England was essentially lily-white. Race was not a problem because there was only one race. Everyone had been born in

England. The Church of England was the State religion so neither was this a problem for most people. At Chelmsford Hall the whole school went to church on Sundays. At Tonbridge the dominant building on campus was the chapel, and the whole school started each day with a service in chapel, and on Sundays went to both morning and evening services. The Headmaster at the time was still an ordained priest. The few boys who were not Church of England were permitted to attend a church in town with their parents' permission. Studying the bible, going through the catechism, and being confirmed were simply a part of school life. I accepted it along with Math and French. Over the years this has now changed as more and more immigrants have come in from former colonies and through the European Union. Religion particularly has become a problem as significant numbers of moslems have taken up residency, especially in the inner cities. This has not affected Tonbridge and other private schools, but has changed the kinds of issues that public schools confront.

In America religion has not been the issue, partly because America is so religiously diverse, partly because of the constitutional separation of church and State. It is true that religious groups are always trying to insert religion into the syllabus in one way or another, most recently by claiming that creationism should be taught, but so far they have been unsuccessful. Race on the other hand has always been a problem, and continues to be so. When ACT looked at the 2005 scores on their test of advanced or college-ready reading skills it found that overall only 50% of high school graduates met the benchmark score, which is a problem by itself of course when you remember that the ACT is typically taken only by students thinking of going to college. Broken down by race the figures were 59% for whites, 54% for asian-americans, 36% for native-americans, 33% for Hispanics, and 21% for African-americans. Recently NAEP (The National Assessment of Educational Progress) published the results of the 2007 writing assessment. While the scores in all groups had improved since 1988 (more students are staying in school), the gap between the various groups had not. 8th grade whites outscored blacks 164 to 141 and outscored Hispanics 164 to 142. The 12th grade results were similar, whites outscoring blacks 159 to 137 and Hispanics 159 to 139. Because good jobs are linked to educational achievement the result is a class structure by race, with whites occupying the top of the occupational structure, and blacks the bottom. A good example of this struck me when my wife was receiving care at the Hospital of the University of Pennsylvania in Philadelphia. The cancer building was a rectangle of about 10 stories. When you entered Admissions on the first floor the staff was almost entirely black. As you went up the elevator on to the medical floors, the staff became almost entirely white, with a sprinkling of Asians. This was 16 years ago and I doubt it has changed.

Recently I was thinking of moving to Houston in Texas, which is a very large city with a diverse population. I looked at schools on the State website and found that I could describe the schools simply by looking at their average ACT scores. Schools which had large minority populations or large poverty populations had lower ACT scores. Schools with high average ACT scores were either private, specialized, or in the suburbs. In Texas where I lived, half the students were Hispanic as I have said and hailed from Mexico. As a group they scored lower than whites, but it was significant that the poorest students of both races did equally poorly. When we moved to rural Alabama recently we came to a small town in an economically depressed part of that State. There are 3,000 residents and blacks make up 63% of this population. The unemployment rate is 21% and 33.4% live below the poverty level. The local high school has 484 students, of whom 9 are white. Where do the other white children go? There are three private schools, which are almost entirely white. My daughter goes to one of them. In other words, the schools are almost totally segregated. I could not see sending her to the public school where she would be the only white girl! This pattern of predominantly black public schools and predominantly white private schools is a common pattern throughout the South. It is echoed by the fact that there are white churches and black churches, which are also entirely segregated, and white and black social clubs. My children are currently playing in a community softball tournament. There are five white teams, and two black teams. It is as if there are two societies. People make choices in their lives, and one of the choices they make is with whom they wish to consort. The problem is not segregation per se, but the fact that blacks disproportionately belong to the lower class, and the culture of the lower class is predominantly anti-education. Education is a middle class value.

There is a black middle class of course. There are two black attorneys, and some black owned businesses, and because the County is predominantly black, the County Commissioners have a black majority, who tend to vote as a block. The public school system of course is all-black, and this includes nearly all the administrators and teachers, but this has little effect on the lower class as a group. 75% of the students in the local public school are in the vocational track, and the school's average ACT score is low. If schools are seen as change agents which move children from poverty to middle income, it is not happening here, nor, obviously, is it happening to any significant extent anywhere else.

Attitudes, Values, and Culture

"Attitude is everything." Anon.

Children come to school with a set of attitudes which they carry with them from home. Some children have been told that school is great, that school is important, that teachers are wonderful people who should be respected. Some children have been told that they have to go, that is the law, that they should do what the teacher tells them to do otherwise they will get into trouble. Some children are told that school is a bore, that one should have a good time, that sports are more important than academics, and that teachers do not care about you. These messages may come from their parents, from their siblings, from their peers, or from what they see on television. Obviously children learn much better when they want to be at school, when they understand that learning involves a little work, and when their family supports education.

I have no memory of the first school I attended in Nelson, Wales. My father had sent me there at age six to live with my aunt in the house in which he had grown up. War had just been declared with Germany and as I have said, the government had asked families who lived in London to evacuate their children to the countryside. My father was a banker, and his work kept him in London, so away I went. I attended the local public school which he had attended when he was growing up. My aunt had been a teacher there, so doubtless would have emitted positive messages about education in general and the school in particular. The school was a typical building of the period, set in an asphalt playground at the end of the village's main street. I have no memories of my classes, but I have vivid memories of the Welsh hymns that we used to sing at the beginning of each school day; of fights between the boys and the girls during recess – the girls always won as they lacked any sense of chivalry- and the headmaster, a Mr. Llewellyn, a tall, stooping man in a three piece suit with watch chain and horn rimmed glasses, who used to pass our house every day on his way to the station.

When my father sent me to Chelmsford Hall I had no idea what to expect. I was a little Welsh boy, small for my age, suddenly sent away to live among a bunch of upper middle class strangers in a manor house in the country. I retain vivid memories of being put on the train with a bunch of strange boys, wearing my new uniform, and fighting to restrain my tears. But it would never have occurred to me to resist. I must have trusted my father's judgment. The culture of the school was very much what one would want from a school – high standards, love of learning, a sense of being part of a large group all of whom had the same attitudes and values. I found out that I was intelligent and had no problem developing my acintel. I won prizes, and a scholarship to Tonbridge. Tonbridge was a bigger, better Chelmsford Hall. The same attitudes and values held sway. There was no resistance to learning, to homework, to proper behavior, to a sense of proceeding along a meaningful path to a positive end, namely university, a good job at the end of it all, and a place at the upper level of society.

Compare the values I was bombarded with and the values that Ronnie grew up with. He went to school, it was the law. The school was built like a prison. The first person one met at the door was a police officer, the first object a steel gate. There was no support at home for doing homework, and no expectation of good grades. The students were mostly poor and all black, and few had expectations of going to college. Many simply dropped out, totally uninterested in what the school had to offer. The main job of the teachers was to maintain discipline before they could make any attempt to teach. Some of the teachers could not even write simple clear English. It was a school but the predominant culture was anti-intellectual.

The youngsters who lived at Hutton Poplars attended the local public school. It was not a positive experience for them. They had two strikes against them: they were branded because they were at Hutton Poplars, and they were out of their environment. They were poor kids living in a middle class world. All they wanted was to get back to their familiar haunts in the East End. Leslie, for all his talent and unusual tastes, learned nothing at school and was lost when he tried to go to art school later on. He had never learnt to learn. Learning is very much a middle class attribute.

It is well established in America that many black students have a negative view of schooling and academic intelligence. Ronnie's peers thought that education sucked. Given that for most people education remains the path to a better life, children who do not understand the importance of doing well in school doom themselves. Until this attitude changes they will remain at the bottom of society and, you might say, rightly so. The problem is that it is initially not the fault of the students who are simply reflecting the way they have been reared.

Motivation

"Genius is one per cent inspiration, ninety-nine per cent perspiration."
Thomas Edison.

To do well requires the motive to do well. Many people have talents, which is nice, but the talents seldom amount to anything unless they are worked at. No matter the great body you are born with, you will never be a great athlete if you are not willing to train. No matter the brain you are born with, you will never be a great student unless you are willing to study. It is of little value to be intelligent if you do not do your homework. The striking thing about Jamie in Texas was his motivation. As he said to me, he wanted to learn, he wanted to know. That plus the support he received from his parents and from the teachers, and his basic intelligence, allowed him to gain entrance to one of the elite universities in the country. My son is a talented pianist, and studied for years with a professor at the University of Texas, but he resisted practicing, and unless you practice you will never be really good. What is true of the piano is true of everything else.

Motivation basically comes from knowing what you want to do. You have to have a goal. I remember a student at Tonbridge who at age sixteen told me that he wanted to manage a fleet of oil tankers.

I have no idea where that goal came from, but twenty years later he was managing British Petroleum's fleet. Jamie knew that he wanted to work in information technology. He carried his computer with him wherever he went, and at an early age was writing game programs. By contrast I personally had no idea what I wanted to do. At Tonbridge I studied French, German, and Russian. This was not because I had an interest in languages but because I did not have an interest in anything specific, and there was a need for more students in the program. As it happened my chief teacher, Alfred Foster, was wonderful, and made languages exciting and interesting. I enjoyed reading Moliere, Corneille, Racine, Schiller, and Goethe, and I loved touring the continent, but I was never a good linguist. I found this out when I went to Cambridge, and at the end of my first year I switched to law. I was not particularly interested in law either, but I had to do something and law seemed as good as anything else.

I never made any attempt to practice law, but instead tried banking (my father's profession). I worked for Lloyd's Bank in Paris, and I loved living in that city, but banking bored me. I sailed to America and obtained a job with Time Magazine, but I found nothing there to excite me. I hitch-hiked through South America and came back to Europe. A friend who was a priest suggested I go to Naples, Italy to help a priest there who was working with abandoned children. His program was called the Casa dello Scugnizzo. For the first time in my life I found something that I really enjoyed doing. I found it meaningful. I felt I was doing something worthwhile. I was motivated! After a short while the priest put me in daily charge of the program. I worked seven days weeks, from morning to night. I enjoyed being a boss. I was motivated, although I did not recognize it at the time. When I went to Cambridge the whole idea of studying anything like how to be a boss was regarded as worthless. I had been a school prefect at Tonbridge but it never occurred to me that I was being a boss. As a consequence of going to Naples I eventually ended up developing a program for people with mental retardation of all ages in Pennsylvania. I spent 22 years growing the program, and ended up with 850 employees and an annual budget of 32 million. I enjoyed every minute of it.

Many students have no idea what they want to do. According to

ACT about 50% of college applicants in America do not know what they want to study.

When I went to Tonbridge no one thought to sit down with me to talk seriously about what I wanted to do. This has now changed, and a lot of energy is spent on career guidance. But at the current time neither in Texas nor in Alabama do the schools offer any assistance to students in this matter. It is assumed somehow that students and/ or their families will find their way, but this does not always happen. Colleges have taken up this slack and now all have career guidance offices, but this should surely be done in high school before you waste time and money studying subjects in which you have no interest.

A persistent complaint by students is that they do not see any point in taking many of the courses that are offered in high school, whether they be history, mathematics, or nineteenth century English novels. They have a point. They might be more enthusiastic if they could see a connection with their life goals, but this is impossible to see if they have no life goals. Middle class children on the whole accept classes simply because they accept the whole idea of education as being valuable in its own right, as well as being a path to a better life.

In America there is a tremendous emphasis on sports, both in private and public schools. Even relatively small schools have impressive gyms and football stadiums, things which are non-existent in England. Even at Tonbridge if you wanted to watch a game you stood or sat on the grass. When I questioned this emphasis on sports with the superintendent in Texas he told me that it was the only way to keep kids in school. More recently in Alabama I was given the same story. The school my daughter attends has a problem obtaining students as another private school in a nearby town is larger and therefore has a better sports program. Many children who live in our little town take the bus to go to that school simply for that reason. The principal told me that in his opinion he needed to establish a scholarship to attract athletes to his school so the sports teams would start winning. Not only do you have to have a team, but you have to have a team that wins.

Ronnie's main motive was to get out of the ghetto. He did not want to end up like his brothers and sisters. My wife and I showed him how to do that, but he still had to be motivated to do it.

Mental Stability

Recently a government-appointed medical panel in America urged that teenagers be routinely screened for signs of depression, stating that nearly two million teens are affected by this debilitating condition. But mental health issues are not confined to high school. They can begin in kindergarten. A recent study in England reported that young children were anxious, badly behaved, stressed, depressed, and obsessed with the cult of celebrity. It stated that there was a decline in mutual respect for fellow pupils and teachers. It described a world for primary school pupils that was bleak and threatening, with pervasive anti-social behavior among older children, and urban neighborhoods full of knives, drugs, and guns. An earlier UNICEF report had found that children in the United Kingdom were the unhappiest in the western world as a result of the tensions brought about by the lack of social cohesion in the country.

In 2007 it was reported in England that the number of prescriptions written for drugs for depression and other mental health disorders for children under the age of 16 had quadrupled over the last decade. Meanwhile in America it was reported that from 2000 to 2003 the prescription of drugs for ADHD for children under five contributed to a 23% per cent increase for all children. In the same period the use of antidepressants rose by 21% and the use of drugs for autism and other conduct disorders increased by 71%. But the most startling figure was that the use of drugs for ADHD for children under five increased by 369%! In other words, if you cannot manage their behavior, drug them!

In the schools I attended at the time I attended them these issues did not exist. No one had a problem sitting at their desk, in paying attention to the teacher, in doing their homework. My memory is that the vast majority of students were happy. As far as I know this is still true of Tonbridge and similar schools. ADHD of course had not been discovered, but then none of its symptoms were present. I cannot imagine any student in the schools I attended attacking their teacher, or even being rude to them. Students did not fight each other, or wantonly destroy property. The problems that I listed above are largely a function of the lower classes. At Hutton Poplars children exhibited all these behaviors, but of course they were a different kind of select group. They did not want to be there, they did not share a culture with their teachers or their staff, they came from broken families, and they had little reason to behave well.

In 2008 Dr. Mary Bousted, the head of the Association of Teacher and Lecturers in Britain was quoted as saying that "there is rising concern that more and more children are coming to school unable to learn because their lives are so dispirited and they are under stress." Professor Robin Alexander of Cambridge University stated that primary schools were engulfed by a wave of anti-social behavior, materialism, and the cult of celebrity. The list of possible causes was as follows:

- The government's rigid system of testing and its constant drive to reach targets.
- Lessons that are boring.
- Teachers who had to spend too much time teaching to the test.
- Compulsory homework.
- The death of fun and play in primary schools.
- The pressure on schools to do well on league tables.
- The constant interference of politicians.
- The loss of childhood.
- The sterile and often fearful environment outside of school – traffic, the lack of safe play areas, rubbish, graffiti, gangs, drugs.
- Marital breakdown and family instability.
- The constant distraction and possible harmful effects of television, ipods, cell phones, and other gadgets.
- Widespread poverty.
- Cultural and religious confusion.

Having listed all that it should be pointed out that much of it applies to poor, urban settings. I am still in touch with Tonbridge, and as I have said, it still seems to be much the same as it was fifty years ago. The school in Texas will have changed over the years however, largely because of the influx of Hispanics, the prevalence of poverty in both races, and the disappearance of meaningful work. Still Texas was an improvement over its urban equivalents. One of the teachers told me she had moved from Uvalde, the nearest big town, which was 45 miles away, because she could not cope with the students – mostly Hispanic

– who were rude and hostile with no interest in learning. She said that many of them simply sat at the back of the classroom and went to sleep. She accepted that because it was preferable to their being awake and causing problems. She found the small rural school wonderful after that. It is true that most of the students were very pleasant. The school in fact won plaudits from a survey in a national magazine. It would seem that rural poor Hispanics, for whatever reason, are pleasanter than urban poor Hispanics.

Nevertheless many of the children were on behavioral drugs of one kind or another. Homework was almost non-existent, not because of any positive reason, but because the teachers did not think it would be done. Many of the children were very overweight, the result of sitting in front of the TV and eating snacks and a culture which supported the consumption of fast fatty food. Even poor children had electronic gadgets. There was the same testing culture as in England, and the same league tables. A number of the children had mental health problems, not easily dealt with in that setting, far from anything that could be called a mental health clinic.

Anti-social behavior is a problem in both countries. Recently in England politicians, including the prime minister, have argued that anti-social children should be and can be identified in kindergarten, and that programs should be put in place at an early age to try to deal with these children before they become a real problem to themselves and others. This is more easily discussed than achieved and does not answer the question of why so many children are mentally and behaviorally challenged in the first place.

I would also argue that if a child has a true mental illness which interferes with his learning (as well as many other things) that the school is not the place to treat him. Teachers are not therapists in the professional sense of the word, and do not have time to be therapists even in a non-professional sense. Teachers should focus on teaching.

Special Needs Children

Just as the number of children with mental health issues has grown over the years so has the number of children identified as having special needs. In 2009 20.5% of children in England were so identified. These are children who have problems with speech, with reading, and with behavior. Once again there is a need to make sure that the specific need is real, and that it can be met within the normal school setting. Given that children with mental retardation (or intellectual disability as it is now called in America) are not included in this figure, the rates are truly alarming. Is it possible that 1 in 5 children are suffering from specific genuine disabilities, which interfere with their learning, or is the disability itself learned, the result of a developmental experience which is not conducive to learning. It is a difficult question, and the answer is unclear at this time.

Other Countries

On International Tests of various kinds American and English children typically score in the middle of the pack. One country which does very well is Finland. On the most recent Program for International Student Assessment, the Finns scored first overall, first in science, and near the top in Reading and Math. For instance it scored 563 on Science, compared to 515 for the United Kingdom and 489 for America, and 548 on Math, compared to 495 for the United Kingdom and 474 for America. It is worth asking why. Outsiders who have visited Finnish schools remark on two things: well-trained teachers and responsible children. Teaching is a valued profession in Finland, so that there are many applicants for open positions. New teachers have to have master's degrees. The salaries are no higher than in America or in England, but they have more freedom to pick books and to customize their lessons to the needs of the students and to their own teaching style. In other words, they enjoy some measure of professional freedom. But perhaps the most important factors are that everyone is a Finn and speaks Finnish – there is little immigration and Finnish is the only language, whereas in America about 8% of the students are learning English as a second language; the gap between the rich and the poor is far less than in America and England; funding is roughly equal across schools; there is far less difference between the poorest performing schools and the best performing; and there is a dropout rate of between 4 and 10%, compared to the rate of 25% in America. For the last three years of high school students are separated on the basis of their grades, with about 53% staying in an academic track and the rest entering vocational schools. College is free. Finally there is far less poverty, and Finland has a small population of somewhat over five million.

Other countries which scored above America and England included South Korea, Japan, Switzerland, Australia, Canada, Netherlands, Iceland, France, New Zealand, and the Czech Republic. American educators fly over to see what makes these countries better, but there seems to be no clear explanation. In 2007 McKinsey, an international consultancy firm, had a look. They claimed that the high-scoring countries do three things: hire the best teachers; get the best out of those teachers; and intervene as soon as an individual students shows signs of dropping behind. I shall have to more to say about this later.

Chapter Two

What Do Parents Bring To Education?

"Do parents have any important long-term effects on the development of their child's personality? This article examines the evidence and concludes that the answer is no." Harris.

"Group socialization theory makes this prediction: that children would develop into the same sort of adults if we left their lives outside the home unchanged – left them in their schools and neighborhoods – but switched all the parents around." Harris.

"The thought that all this love that I'm pouring into him counts for nothing is too terrible to contemplate." A parent.

Do Parents Matter?

In 1995 Judith Rich Harris published an article, and followed it up in 1998 with a book, arguing that parents have little effect on their child's development, that it is the child's peer group that is important. However it should be remembered that parents give birth to the child, provide the child with its genes, locate the child in the social structure, pay the bills, and have the child almost all to themselves for at least a few years. So I would like to start by looking at what the child gets from its parents before it is placed in day care, head start, or school, before, in other words, it has a peer group.

The First Years

A child gets its genes from its father and mother, and those genes have important effects for the whole of the child's life. Intelligence, however defined, is partly inherited. Skin color, which is completely genetically determined, has important effects in how one is regarded, and how one regards oneself, especially in America, but increasingly so in England. As knowledge of the brain increases it seems that more and more components are genetically determined. Those genetic components are not changeable. However these genes play out in their interaction with the environment as the child grows to an adult, the fact is that they initially come from the parents. Genetically it matters to whom you are born. But it also matters socially to whom you are born.

Parents provide the child with its initial social status. Parents may be rich or poor or anywhere in between. Children who are born poor tend to stay poor, for a variety of reasons. A study at London University revealed that the overwhelming factor in how well children do in school is not what type of school they attend, but their social class, but of course schools reflect the segment of society they serve. The schools that come at the top of the league tables are the middle and upper class schools. Exactly the same thing is apparent in America. A child's address predicts his educational achievement. The study found that whatever their background, children do better the more 'middle class' the school they attend, and that more than 50% of a school's performance is accounted for by the social background of its students. But because where students live is also a function of social status, middle class families are served by middle class schools, and lower class families are served by lower class schools.

Parents also provide children with their culture, their language, and their religion. All these elements have effects on a child's educational progress. In Texas many of the students are not only poor, but many of them are Hispanic and speak Spanish at home. They come to a school where all instruction is in English, and where only one of the faculty is Hispanic and she teaches Spanish of all things! In English class they study Shakespeare, usually Romeo and Juliet. Needless to say, their parents are of little use to them if it comes to helping them with their homework or their comprehension of Elizabethan English. Parents rarely come to the school unless there is a problem. At Hutton Poplars the residents were almost all from the lower class, while the staff were from the middle class. The parents of course had no effect on the school, but their children still shared their culture, rather than the culture of the school. Moreover they enjoyed the company of a well-established peer group When I was growing up England was all-white and everybody was either church of England, Roman Catholic, or one of a variety of Protestant faiths. Since that time England has changed dramatically, with thousands of immigrants coming not only from previous colonies, but also from the European Union. The result is that there are now conflicts not only between the classes, but also between racial and religious groups. There are now lots of students for whom English is a second language.

In order to put all of this in context let me quote from an article, published in 1991, by Urie Bronfenbrenner, which I think is one of the best short introductions to the subject of child development that I have ever read. He starts off by quoting a paragraph from a Unicef study:

"It has long been accepted that good health and nutrition support the psychological and social development of the young child. Less widely recognized are the more recent findings that developmentally sensitive interaction with a child, namely interaction which satisfies the child's need to grow socially, psychologically, and cognitively, has a direct and measurable impact on the physical health of the child."

He lists three propositions which need to exist for a child to grow in a normal and healthy manner. Let me quote the first of these.

Proposition One: "A child requires participation in progressively more complex reciprocal activity, on a regular basis, over an extended period in the child's life, with one or more persons with whom the child develops a strong, mutual, irrational, emotional attachment and who is committed to the child's well-being and development, preferably for life." Bronfenbrenner goes on to stress that this interaction is a two-way street, with the child being a leader as well as a follower.

Traditionally, and initially, of course the person has been the child's mother. When I went to school you were either a Freudian or a Skinnerian, an analyst or a behaviorist. Either way it was assumed that the child's experience in the birth family 'developed' the child. For the child to develop normally he had to be treated properly. Bettelheim was an extreme example of this approach. He argued for instance that autism in a child was the result of the child having a refrigerator mother. He blamed the mother. If only the mother had been warmer the condition could have been avoided. This has now been shown to be nonsense. Autism is the result of a genetic defect. It is still tragic, but it is not the fault of the mother. Skinner has also lost his reputation. His assumption that one could take any child and mould that child through a series of reinforcements has not held up.

It is nevertheless reasonable to argue that development requires interaction with other human beings, and initially those human beings are the parents. Children need to be fed, clothed, and washed. They need to be picked up and held. They need to be talked to. They need to be read to. They need to be communicated with.

One of the striking developments in the modern world is the degree to which the child-mother link, which not long ago used to be thought all-important, has been fractured. The Casa and Hutton Poplars were full of children who had been separated from their parents. Many of them were angry, but it was difficult to know whether their anger came from this separation, or whether their anger was there to begin with. Many of the children however were very happy and loving. They were not mentally disturbed. The children who were aggressive, who broke windows, who threw food at other children, and who were on the path to a life of crime, were in the minority.

It is important to remember that even in today's world a child is born to a couple of parents, although how long the parents remain a couple, and how long they raise the child together is another question. P.D.James, in her autobiography, talks about the world in which she grew up in the twenties and thirties in England:

"For the whole of my schooldays, both in primary school and at the High School in Cambridge, I never knew a child whose parents were either separated or divorced. No doubt this fact hid many wretchedly unhappy marriages and some that for the wife were little more than institutionalized slavery. But for the stoically enduring there were compensations. Couples, knowing that they were yoked together for life, frequently made the best of what they had. Those who were able to survive the more turbulent years of youth and middle age often found in each other a reassuring and comforting companionship in old age. They had a far smaller expectation of happiness, admittedly, and a far lesser tendency to regard happiness as a right. All our brightly minted social reforms, the sexual liberation since the war, the guilt-free divorce, the ending of the stigma of illegitimacy, have had their shadow side. Today we have a generation of children more disturbed, more unhappy, more criminal, indeed more suicidal than in any previous era. The sexual liberation of adults has been bought at a high price and it is not the adults who have paid it."

I grew up in a similar world, a world which survived into the fifties. When Princess Margaret wanted to marry the man she loved, the Queen refused to allow it, on the basis that the man had been divorced. The Queen's own children, with one exception, are currently all divorced. In Texas divorce or separation was more common than enduring marriage. The first year I was there at the Homecoming football game the football students and band students were introduced to the crowd, and paraded together with their 'parents'. It was remarkable how many of them paraded with adults who had names different from their own. Often children were being raised by their aunt, or by their grandmother.

Recent data (2009) from England show that the percentage of households comprising the traditional nuclear family – a married couple with children – has fallen to 36% over the past thirty years. 1.66 million children are being raised by an unmarried couple. One in 12 children live through a divorce if their parents are married, but one in two children live through a separation if their parents are not married.

Children take time, energy, and money. It should be noted that the upper classes both in England and America used to leave the raising of their children mostly to their servants and slaves. Children were housed in nurseries, and spent most of their time interacting with their siblings – families were larger than they are today. I think that the image of two devoted parents spending immense amounts of time playing and interacting with their children is a myth. In the days when mothers did not work they certainly spent time with their children – that was their job - but the mere fact that mothers now work when they can, does not seem in and of itself to have destroyed their children.

Having said that it is undeniable that children do need to have someone to interact with as soon as they are out of the womb. Children who are deprived of such interaction do develop problems. But that someone does not have to be a parent. I have spent most of my life looking after other peoples' children. They were separated from their parents for a variety of reasons. Sometimes the parent was a single mother who could not cope, sometimes the father was abusive so the child ran away, sometimes the child was so disabled that the parents gave up, sometimes the child was old enough to get into trouble with the law, sometimes the child was mentally ill. The children were as varied as their backgrounds. Sometimes a child would be highly intelligent, able to talk about their situation, and what to do about it. Sometimes a child would be so angry that any sort of interaction would be rejected. Most of them were responsive once they learned to trust, which sometimes took a while. The main problem, I think, is the loss of a sense of security. If you do not grow up with your parents it is difficult to know who is responsible for you, who you can turn to in case of need. What is a daughter to make of a situation where her mother has a different man in her bed every couple of years? What is a child to do if she does not even know her parents? Even worse, what is a child to do if their parent abuses them?

I do think that a child needs to know that someone cares about them, that they will be there for them if needed. It is an issue of commitment. If you bring a child into this world you should be prepared to give them unconditional love and attention. When I was evacuated to Wales I did not feel that I was being banished because I had done something wrong. I knew that my parents were doing it for my benefit. When they sent me to boarding school I was scared, but I also understood that it was for my benefit. However most of the children I have cared for in my life have been 'sent' to where they lived, and did not believe it was for their benefit, even though they were told it was. Sometimes they had been duly labeled as delinquent, sometimes their parents had given up on them, sometimes their parents had abused them, but in all cases they were not given a choice. One day their home became impossible and they found themselves in an institution, being cared for by a group of strangers, who did not speak their language, and did not share their culture.

While the absence or breakdown of a family can be dealt with if the child is lucky and finds a substitute arrangement, it does seem that the child needs to be raised in an intellectually stimulating environment if he or she is to develop acintel. Nisbett among others emphasizes the degree to which different environments produce different results. If middle class children start moving past lower class children as they both progress through school it must largely be the result of the greater support the middle class child receives in his environment. If asian children do so well when they come to America it must be because of something in their culture.

Bronfenbrenner continues:

Proposition Two: "The child requires the establishment of patterns of progressive interpersonal interaction under conditions of strong mutual attachment which enhance the child's responsiveness to features of his physical, social, and eventually symbolic environment that invite exploration, manipulation, elaboration, and imagination. It is these patterns which enhance the child's psychological growth."

I was fortunate to grow up before the advent of television. In Nelson I would play with the village kids, in the streets, which was where kids played. We would make up games, and explore the local countryside. I remember finding an old abandoned mine shaft – we amused ourselves by throwing stone down it and listening to the echo. It never occurred to us that we might fall in and hurt ourselves. We would play marbles. In the center of the village there was a handball court – it still exists – and we would play ball or watch games. There was a newspaper and candy shop – the owner was reputed to be a witch, so it was a dare to go in there. We would make bows and arrows and try to shoot birds. We would play endless ball games. The village was a playground, full of stuff to do. On Friday nights, when the miners were paid, we would wait outside the pub in the high street to watch the wives come to get their share of the pay before it was drunk. The village policeman was regarded as a friend rather than a foe – after all we all knew him. There was no fear of being kidnapped or abused. The world of the village was our oyster and we explored it to our heart's content. Kids played with other kids, and the physical, social, and symbolic environment was everything around us.

My aunt was obviously not a family but because she had been a teacher she had some familiarity with children. She was well spoken and her favorite program was The Brains Trust. The room in which I slept had books which I could read, including an illustrated encyclopedia on the Great War which I remember to this day. Once a week I was allowed to go to the local cinema where I and my friends sat on wooden benches right in front of the screen. The movie stars of the time were Charles Boyer and Greer Garson. On Sundays we would go to church, and my aunt would take me by bus to the local mountains, where I could jump from rock to rock to my heart's content.

I recently read some remarks by Viv Richards, a famous West Indian cricketer, who deplored the diminished state of that game in the islands. He said that when he was growing up, all the children would spend the evenings playing cricket in the street: now they spent the evenings on a couch in front of the television set.

I agree with Harris that most of development occurs through interaction with other children, rather than with adults. In many ways I had an idyllic childhood, but little of it that I remember was with my family. I went to live in Nelson at age 6. As far as I was concerned my aunt was an old lady – she was in fact 50. As I have said I remember her with some respect – it cannot have been easy for a 50 year old spinster to suddenly have a six year old boy placed with her. I have no memory of being unhappy in the three years I spent with her. At age ten I went to live at Chelmsford Hall, to live with a group of some 40 boys, roughly my age. The Hall's usual location was the town of Eastbourne on England's southern coast across from France, so it too had been evacuated to a mansion in the Somerset countryside, near the town of Wellington. Doubtless when I arrived I had a Welsh lilt to my voice. Doubtless I soon started talking like anyone else. The Headmaster, Colonel Stevens, was one of the nicest men I have ever known, as was Mr. Smith, his head teacher. They were firm, but they were kind. Academic standards were high, but there was lots of free time, and as in Nelson, we created imaginary worlds. We created a pool by damming up a local stream and built a complete imaginary village together with toy cars. Every Sunday we bicycled to church in the morning and went on a long walk through the countryside in the afternoon. I had forty other kids more or less my age to play with.

There were no girls, but I do not remember that any of us saw this as a problem! At that age girls are a nuisance.

Proposition Three: "The establishment and maintenance of patterns of progressively more complex interaction and emotional attachment between caregiver and child depend in substantial degree on the availability and involvement of another adult, a third party who assists, encourages, spells off, gives status to, and expresses admiration and affection for the person caring for the child."

Traditionally of course this has been the father. Once again the breakdown of the nuclear family threatens this relationship. In Texas my wife ran a program called In-School-Suspension. Students were sent there if they got into behavioral trouble in class. Needless to say, the students that she had were not often the cream of the crop. One in particular was very angry with life, and would relieve himself when angry by putting his fist through the wall, and he was angry most of the time. He was not unintelligent, but totally uninterested in schoolwork, and totally incapable of planning his life in any sensible way. His mother was in prison and he lived with an aunt, poor lady, who did what she could. Out of school he hung around with the other semi-delinquent kids. His aunt could not control him, but neither could the school. One of the great problems in the black lower class community in America is the degree to which fathers are not there, physically or psychologically. My wife for a time worked in a deli on South Street in Philadelphia and there were some young black men who worked as janitors. In talking with them my wife discovered that they already had children, that they had no intention of marrying the girls, and that they viewed themselves as responsible fathers if they supplied the girls with diapers for a year!

A major problem in both America and England is the number of children who are born to fathers who take no responsibility for them. In and of itself that does not destroy the child, but it certainly makes the mother's job that much harder, and it makes the developmental prognosis of the child that much more fragile. Mothers frequently simply stay at home with their parents if they can, or find another man. In Texas, a small community, the number of women who bounced from man to man was quite extraordinary. Children survive, but the point is not whether they survive, but whether they would have survived better had there been a father in their life. A lot depends on the father of course. An absent father is better than an abusive father, but a good father is better than an absent father, especially if the absent father offers no support at all. Raising a child is taxing both physically and financially. Good fathers not only support the mother psychologically, but provide an income. It should also be remembered that stepfathers who do not care about the child are frequently worse than an absent father. It is frequently argued that children, especially boys, need male role models, but the evidence is unclear. If Harris in correct, the male role models that boys will emulate are those of their peer group. When the peer group has socially and educationally positive values, as mine did, there is no problem, but when the peer group fosters gang values which are anti-social and anti-educational, of course there are problems.

It is worth thinking precisely what father responsibility means. In a sense, my father was an absent father. At age six I left home to go to Wales, and from that day on only returned home for vacations. In many ways my home became the place I went to, and my school became the place where I felt at home. My image of my father was that of a man who left for work in the morning, came home in the evening, had dinner, and then sat in front of the fire reading Country Life. On Saturdays he would disappear to play golf, the love of his life, and a place where he never took any of his family. On Sundays mother would insist on regular trips to Sheerness, the small seaside town where she had been born and where she still had a sister, and this bored everyone except, I suppose, her. But father did take me to Wales versus England rugby internationals, and to local soccer games. When I became an outstanding student athlete at Tonbridge he would turn up at sporting events to see me run and play. Also of course he paid for everything, and never begrudged me anything I needed. He paid for my trips to Europe, and later on when I was at Cambridge he not only opened an account for me at the local bookseller's, but also one at the liquor store. I never really knew him very well, but I did appreciate him and valued what he did for me. He was certainly responsible, not only to me but also to his family. When my sister had a son she also sent him to Chelmsford Hall and Tonbridge, and my father helped with the expenses. Years later my sister helped with the college expenses of her grand-daughters. Such is the power of family ties and culture.

Location and Culture

Parents also supply the child with its initial social and geographical location, and its initial culture. You start off life as either middle or lower class, and that is where you tend to end. There are of course poor kids who work their way to the top, and there are rich kids who fall to the bottom, but they are the exceptions. There is individual social mobility, both in England and in America, but not as much as one might think. It is much easier to stay in the middle if you start in the middle than it is to move up to the middle if you start at the bottom. In every city there are areas where the poor live, areas where the rich live, and areas that are in-between. It is very difficult for a child born into the middle class to know what it is like to be born poor, and vice versa, except to the extent that they see on television what passes for social life. It is quite possible for a middle class person to pass their life without ever meeting a poor person. Furthermore there is no incentive for the middle class person to cross that divide. Why should he? He is too busy securing his own status to worry about someone else's.

Before television the poor knew very little about the middle class, unless of course they were domestic servants. Television changed that. Everyone on television seems to have lots of money, to live in pleasant suburban houses, and to drive expensive cars. Money literally oozes out of the screen. What is a poor child to make of all this? He can now see how the other people live. He can aspire to that life, but how is he to get there? That is where culture comes in.

It is a fact that people with college degrees earn more than people without. Middle class parents assume that their children will go to college, and plan accordingly, and their children accept college as a fact of life. No one has to persuade them that they need to go. It is different with the lower class. Schools by definition are middle class institutions. They believe in studying, in deferred gratification, in the importance of academic credentials, in respect, and in the value of parental support. Lower class parents too frequently see the school as a foreign entity which does not speak their language, and their children too frequently adopt the same stance.

The power of culture was very clear in Texas. To take an example which has nothing to do with education, when we arrived we decided that in order to get to know some people we would invite them to dinner. So we did this with people whom we thought might make good friends. We assumed that they would invite us back to their house. To our surprise this did not happen. People cheerfully came and ate our food and drank our wine, but we were not invited back except by two families, one which had moved from Michigan, and one which was English! I realized that in the world of Texas, reciprocity simply was not a value. People did not entertain each other in their homes. The various churches served as meeting places, and this was where people socialized. This had nothing to do with people being hostile. It simply never occurred to them to invite us back. It just was not done. Similarly, when I first arrived I was told that the only kids who went on to college were the teachers' kids. The intimation was that this was racist, the teachers being almost all white. In fact the difference was largely cultural. The teachers had all been to college and had degrees, so they knew that it was important that their children go, and therefore made sure that this happened. The Hispanic parents for the most part did not have degrees, did not appreciate their value, and thought that their kids should find work as soon as they left school. The power of these values was made clear as there were a few mothers who despite being poor themselves wanted a better life for their children, and understood that college was the way to go. Their values were reflected in the behavior of their children.

The poor have a different culture from the rich, and nowhere is this more apparent that among the black lower class in America. Look at the way they dress. Now that Obama has been elected President one can reflect what this may means for blacks. I believe it will mean very little. Can you imagine Obama wearing baggy clothing where the crotch of his pants is at knee level, where his shoes are one size too big and unlaced, where his main music is rap? There is a black middle and upper class, and Obama of course belongs to that class, but the problem is in the lower class. There are lower class Asians, and perhaps even lower class Jews, but both the latter cultures value education. My son who is white, middle class, and bright, knows who the best students are. In his view, they are Asians.

Parents who value education will do whatever it takes to ensure that their children receive a good one. Both in England and America schools are regularly ranked and compared to each other, so that parents can make choices. One choice is to send your child to a private school (also ranked), but another option is to live in the right area, that is the area which has the best schools. In England this is compounded by an area being served by a number of schools, and the parents have to submit their choices to the local authority, which means that their child will not necessarily go to their first choice school, but that is another issue. To live in the area with the best schools also takes money however.

If the effects of the lottery of birth is to ever change, then lower class parents have to somehow learn middle class values, even though they do not belong to the middle class by birth. They have to be involved in the life of the school, and they have to ensure that their children take advantage of the many opportunities that are available to them. There was one mother in Texas who did that. She was overweight, she had children by more than one man, she was not married, her income was a mystery but I assumed it came largely from the government, she lived in a trailer, she was loud, she was pushy, and she was intelligent. She had three daughters. She knew that education was important and that it was essential to go to college. She spent time and energy on her daughters, she came and talked at School Board meetings, she knew how to get what she wanted. The result was that her daughters were also motivated. One is now in college, and I assume that the others will go to. Somehow she will make it happen. She knows how.

Chapter Three

What Do Teachers Bring to Education?

"To me education is a leading out of what is already there in the pupil's soul. To Miss Mackay it is a putting in of something that is not there, and that is not what I call education, I call it intrusion." Muriel Spark.

At first sight this might seem like a silly question. Teachers teach. The problem is that some teachers teach better than others, as I am sure everyone will agree. But what does that mean exactly? Let me start by looking at why teachers are so important.

The Importance of Teachers

From the point of view of the student, teachers are education. A student may occasionally see an administrator, hardly ever a bureaucrat, but he spends his whole school life in a classroom with a whole series of adults who are being paid to teach him. If a student fails to learn, the question is whether that is the fault of the student or the fault of the teacher. A recent study in England compared teachers who were ranked in the top twenty five percent to teachers who were ranked in the bottom twenty five percent. The teachers were ranked on a scale which was based on their age, their experience, the number of years in the school, salary status, and whether they had been awarded any leadership allowances. 6500 students were rated on how they performed on national exams in English, math, and science taken at age 16. The study found that students taught by the poorer teachers did significantly worse on the exams. It seems that teachers do matter.

Ideally bad teachers would be fired. After all, it is the student who is the consumer, not the teacher, and therefore no student should be exposed to a poor teacher. Unfortunately firing teachers seems to be a limited option. In England poor teachers are meant to be referred to the General Teaching Council, which has the power to bar failing teachers, but in its seven years of existence only ten teachers have in fact been barred from the profession. Local Councils are legally required to report incompetent teachers, but two thirds of them have never reported a single teacher in ten years. Ten years ago Ofsted (The Office for Standards in Education) estimated that there were between 15 and 17 thousand incompetent teachers in the system (out of 500 thousand total teachers). What this means is that the vast majority of these incompetent teachers are still teaching, and the million or more students they teach are still suffering.

Of course firing staff is never pleasant. Unions will always support the teacher, as frequently will fellow teachers. Principals are often loath to initiate a process which will involve them in lengthy hearings, the end of which is never certain. Recently I met with the current Headmaster of Tonbridge and asked him how he dealt with the problem of incompetent teachers. He said that the trick was not to hire them! He said that building up an outstanding teaching staff was a long process. He agreed that getting rid of teachers was a difficult thing to do, albeit sometimes necessary. His problem was easier than most because the reputation of Tonbridge ensured that he had multiple candidates for any open position. In state schools on the other hand principals frequently have difficulty finding teachers, especially in certain subjects, and especially in schools with difficult students. In 2007 for instance the school superintendent for Guilford County in North Carolina said that teacher turnover was such a problem that in some high-poverty schools principals were hiring new teachers for nearly every class every term. They were offering $10,000 sign-on bonuses, and still had problems. As he said, there were some schools which did not have a single certified math teacher! The reason of course is that the better teachers want to teach better students in the better schools.

In New York City Mayor Bloomberg has managed to institute a program of performance pay, which is an idea which has been discussed for years, but which only recently seems to be gathering traction. Under the plan additional monies will be given to poverty schools which meet certain performance goals. At the same time, Bloomberg wants to measure teachers by their students' performance and improvement, an idea which is likely to meet with significant union resistance. Obama is on record as supporting going in this direction..

Knowledge

The first job of a teacher is to present a specific area of knowledge, and to present it in such a way that the students learn it. So an English teacher teaches English, a math teacher teaches math, and so on. The content depends of course on the age of the students and their grade or form level. When a teacher walks into a classroom for the first time and sees her students before her, she is faced with that challenge: how does she impart that body of knowledge over the next 14 weeks so that at the end of it the students can demonstrate that they are duly taught, and can pass on to the next grade.

Jane Eyre in Charlotte Bronte's novel of the same name is faced with just that challenge:

"This morning, the village school opened. I had twenty scholars. But three of the number can read: none write or cipher. Several knit, and a few can sew a little. They speak with the broadest accent of the district. At present they and I have a difficulty in understanding each other's language. Some of them are unmannered, rough, intractable, as well as ignorant; but others are docile, have a wish to learn, and evince a disposition that pleases me. I must not forget that these coarsely-clad little peasants are of flesh and blood as good as the scions of gentlest genealogy; and that the germs of native excellence, refinement, intelligence, kind feeling, are as likely to exist in their hearts as in those of the best-born. My duty will be to develop these germs: surely I shall find some happiness in discharging that office....I continued the labours of the village-school as actively and faithfully as I could. It was truly hard work at first. Some time elapsed before, with all my efforts, I could comprehend my scholars and their nature. Wholly untaught, with faculties quite torpid, they seemed to me hopelessly dull; and at first sight, all dull alike: but I soon found I was mistaken. There was a difference amongst them as amongst the educated; and when I got to know them, and they me, this difference rapidly developed itself. Their amazement at me, my language, my rules, and ways, once subsided, I found some of these heavy-looking, gaping rustics wake up into sharp-witted girls enough. Many showed themselves obliging, and amiable too; and I discovered amongst them not a few examples of natural politeness, and innate self-respect, as well as of excellent capacity, that won my good-will and my admiration. These soon took a pleasure in doing their work well; in keeping their persons neat; in learning their tasks regularly; in acquiring quiet and orderly manners. The rapidity of their progress. in some instances, was even surprising; and an honest and happy pride I took in it: besides, I began personally to like some of the best girls; and they liked me.....these could already read, write, and sew; and to them I taught the elements of grammar, geography, history, and the finer kinds of needlework. I found estimable characters amongst them – characters desirous of information, and disposed for improvement.."

For a teacher, life has not changed very much. When Charlotte Bronte lived, middle class women married well if they could, or became housekeepers or governesses – all three Bronte sisters were governesses and none of them married. In Charlotte's day, teachers, especially at the primary level, were expected to teach multiple subjects. Teachers were almost all female, as they still are in primary schools in both England and America. It does not in fact seem too demanding to expect a teacher to be able to teach reading, writing, and arithmetic in the initial years. A recent report in England however claims that one of the reasons English primary school children do so poorly is that the teachers are poorly trained. The report said that primary school teachers in England are among the worst qualified in Europe, needing only C grades in math and English in the General Certificate of Education exams, which are taken usually at age 16. What this means, according to Professor Burghes who was one of the authors of the study, is that the teachers do not have an adequate knowledge base. The further challenge facing teachers is their ability to transfer their knowledge into the heads and minds of their students, and if they themselves are weak, how can they possibly do that?

In 2007 Robert Pianta of the University of Virginia published a study entitled 'Opportunities to Learn in America's Elementary Classrooms'. He and his colleagues observed 2,500 classrooms in 400 school districts across the United States. They found that the typical child had a 1-in-14 chance of learning in a rich, supportive environment. Fifth graders spent 91 percent of their time listening to the teacher or working alone, usually on low-level worksheets. Three out of four classrooms were dull, bleak places, devoid of any emphasis on critical reasoning or problem-solving skills. His study is depressing to read.

At Chelmsford Hall, which was a small school, the main teachers taught multiple subjects at multiple levels. There was a part-time lady who taught French, and another part-time lady who taught music. My nephew started in a village school, where teachers taught multiple subjects at multiple levels. The knowledge required to teach in elementary schools does not seem exacting, but nevertheless it is crucial that the basis is laid for what is to follow. The task after all is to ensure that the students learn the basics of the various subjects, on which they can then build as they progress to high school. It is in high school that the knowledge base, or lack of it, truly becomes a problem. The task after all, in this day and age, is to prepare many students to go to college, which means that the teachers need to be expert in their specific discipline and that when students graduate they are college ready. As is well known, this does not always happen.

One problem is that in both America and England the brightest college graduates do not enter the teaching profession. Recently the head of admissions for Cambridge University said that children who attend state schools are being handicapped academically by poor quality teachers. He went on to state that it was very clear that what made the most difference to a young person was the quality of their teachers. When asked why bright college graduates did not enter the profession, he said that good graduates who had other choices would run a mile before becoming a teacher due to bureaucracy, pupil behavior, and stress. Another report by a former head of school standards in England pointed out that South Korea, Finland, Singapore, and Hong Kong all managed to attract high level graduates to their schools, while in America only the bottom 33% go into teaching, with the figures in

England being not much better. The problem is compounded by the fact that the better teachers gravitate to the better schools, and the worst schools have not only the worst students but the worst teachers.

A major problem of course is the low quality of college education departments. It is well established that Colleges of Education in America have lower intellectual standards than other colleges, and so tend to attract students with lower scores. An education degree is regarded as an easy degree. I remember at the College of New Jersey, which had been a teacher training college until quite recently, I was amazed when I found out the low scores that graduates were obtaining on the Graduate Record Exams, and these were the brighter students! Overall, the academic standards at the College were lower than those at Tonbridge, and presumably at similar American high schools.

David Steiner, a professor of education at Boston University, caused a stir in 2003 when he announced that after reviewing more that 200 course outlines in16 prestigious universities he found that teacher preparation at these schools was at best uneven and at worst intellectually thin and stressed a particular ideological approach rather than solid learning. In 2006 Arthur Levine, a former president of Teachers College, Columbia University, looked at colleges of education and described the programs as 'unruly and chaotic' and lacking a standard approach to preparing teachers. He affirmed that colleges of education had lower admissions standards and lower graduation standards. It does not say much for the profession of education if those institutions which teach teachers are so poor.

Dr. Levine argued that education programs should be made into professional schools, focusing on what it takes to actually teach a variety of students presenting a whole range of challenges in a typical classroom setting. It is interesting, for instance, that no one argues that university professors should have to be certified teachers. Why? Presumably because university professors are meant to be scholars first, and teachers second, and furthermore deal with students who theoretically at least want to be in their classroom and want to learn. The task of the professor is to be an expert in his field. Equally at Tonbridge and Chelmsford Hall the teachers were not certified to teach, nor did anyone ever suggest they should be —as a private school they did not have to be. Teachers were hired because they had good degrees from good universities in the subject matter they were going to teach. Because Tonbridge was a high school preparing students to go to good universities it was assumed that they needed to prepare students to work at that level, and in order to do that they needed to know what that level was, and be fluent at that level. Teachers need to be more knowledgeable than their students. One of my vivid memories from Tonbridge is sitting around with teachers and listening to them make jokes in latin! Chelmsford Hall was also private, and therefore certification there was also meaningless, but it was a primary school, and therefore the level of knowledge of a teacher did not have to be as high as at Tonbridge, but equally they had to teach more than one subject, and they had to prepare their students to function on the academic level of a Tonbridge.

I would argue that all teachers at all high schools should have degrees in their subject, and not in education per se. When you take a degree within a college of education you are required to take numerous courses which have only a very tenuous link to a subject area, and of course the more extraneous courses you take, the fewer courses you take in your discipline. If teachers at private schools do not have to be certified and do not have to graduate from schools of education in order to be certified, why do teachers in state schools have to be? A study of 10,000 New York City teachers found that there was no relationship between what they had to do to be certified and their ability to raise student test scores. Why then do we continue to insist on certifying teachers? The reason surely is that colleges of education within universities are large and significant income generators and lobby vigorously for their continued existence.

The problem is that while it is reasonably clear what the content of the any subject area should be, what a math teacher should know about math for instance, there is little agreement on what kind of program produces a good math teacher, especially a good teacher in the context of an inner city state school, a math teacher who can actually successfully teach math to students in that setting. In 2008 the National Mathematics Advisory Panel in America published a report. On the one hand it found that effective math teachers in the elementary grades accounted for 12 to 14 percent of variation in student math achievement, but on the other hand found that it could not determine what credentials or training contributed to this. It found that certification made no difference, but that teacher content knowledge did make a difference at the high school level, but not at the elementary level. The question is whether there is an educational program at the college level which can teach potential teachers how to successfully teach students who do not want to be taught, who are bored stiff with school, and see education as irrelevant. At this moment this does not happen.

Ability to Teach

You can be very bright, high in acintel, an expert in your field, and still be a poor teacher. That is known. There were poor teachers at Tonbridge. One who I remember to this day was a man who taught math, and specifically calculus. He had a first class degree from Cambridge, and I have no doubt that he knew his subject matter: what he did not know what how to get it from his head into my head. I had been outstanding at math up to the time I came to his class, and my experience with him completely turned me off the field – in fact I decided that I must be stupid. Years later I found myself in a class with a professor at Temple University studying statistics, which is not a subject guaranteed to fill most people with excited enthusiasm, but the teacher was so good, so turned on by his subject, that I found myself getting excited about it too. I went back and took a course in calculus, and found that I could understand it quite well.

Recent studies in England indicate clearly that bad teachers produce bad students. For instance 73000 students were tested in vocabulary, reading, and math from the time they started school and for the following six years. Children whose classes were in the bottom 16 percent in their first year as measured by student progress were performing worse than average six years later, while those who attended classes that were at the top were performing better than average at the later date. Peter Tymms, professor of education at Durham University, pointed out that the effect is cumulative, so that if one bad teacher is followed by another the child starts dropping even further behind. Professor Dylan Williams of the Institute of Education in London went even further. He claimed that children in the most effective classrooms learn in six months what students in an average classroom learn in a year, and that students in the least effective classrooms will take two years.

The problem of course is how to ensure that every teacher in every classroom is a teacher with the ability to teach kids. In America the Leave No Child Behind legislation mandates that teachers be 'highly qualified', whatever that means. This is easier said that done. It certainly does not mean that they can teach. For one thing there are just not enough physics and math teachers. For another thing there are just not enough teachers period. As I said, a recent report in England claimed that there were 17000 unqualified teachers, many of them immigrants, who are hired because of the lack of qualified staff. All that they have to do to obtain a position is to pass a criminal check. Needless to say students from poor homes are more likely to be taught by an unqualified teacher than students from richer homes.

An additional problem is that it seems unclear what highly qualified actually means. In America to meet the standard a teacher of a core subject must have an appropriate license from the State and demonstrate knowledge of the subject taught. Highly qualified comes to mean simply that a teachers has the correct knowledge, but says nothing about the possession of classroom skills or the ability to actually change students. It is much simpler to measure whether a person has taken courses than whether they can teach others. It is true that would-be teachers have to student-teach as part of their program, but very few students are failed through this process, although arguably it is the most important part. One of the problems is that student-teaching comes towards the end of a program, and colleges are loath to fail students at this juncture. The result is that you can be classified as a highly qualified teacher and in fact be totally incompetent.

I think that a major problem is that good teachers are born, not made. I realize that this is a challenging statement to make, but the more I have thought about it, the more I am convinced that it is so. Some people have the ability, and some do not, and I do not think that you can train a poor teacher to be a good teacher except on a very superficial level. It is no different than that personality characteristic which fosters good classroom management. Wherever I have worked there are some people who are good leaders (which is what a teacher has to be) and some (most I would say) who are not. When I asked my daughter recently what she thought of her teachers (and she is very perceptive) she said, well so-and-so is very bright and knows his subject, but he cannot teach, and so-and-so may know the subject, but cannot control the classroom, and so forth. She does not say that one is a good teacher and one is not, but breaks the issue down by what she thinks are the important categories. When I ran LifePath which consisted in multiple programs each of which required a supervisor or teacher or director, selecting people for these roles was not so much a function of what they knew so much as a function of whether they could take a bunch of people and organize them appropriately. This was done by looking at what they had done up to that point, which was a much better indicator than any college degree.

It is clear that there are many things to help the beginning teacher, from how to manage individual students to how to manage a classroom, but I would argue that most of these things are best learned in situ, and that the place to learn how to teach is in the school classroom with students, and not in a college classroom with a professor. In many ways teaching is a craft and like all crafts is best learned from a master through an apprenticeship. I would argue that a would-be teacher should therefore obtain a degree in the subject matter which he or she is interested in teaching, and then spend a year working with an existing teacher in an existing school.

I might add that would-be teachers are taught in most of their courses by ex-teachers who have obtained the appropriate credentials to move up to the college level, but this of course is no guarantee that they know how to teach kids, and may in fact be an indicator of a desire not to teach kids, which is why they want to 'ascend' to the college level.

The Teacher as Motivator

Teaching a bright kid who wants to learn is a joy. Teaching kids who do not want to learn and who therefore constantly misbehave, is not a joy: it is an overwhelming task. I believe that all teachers need to be motivators, that is they need to love their subject and be able to show that love to their students, so that the students in turn can understand why it is worth making an effort to study the subject. To be a motivator a teacher needs to absolutely believe in the value of what they are doing. Frequently one reads that students are bored with school, which in my mind means that they have had too many teachers who are boring. I had a professor at Temple whose idea of teaching was to come to class with copies of his notes on some topic, and then spend the time literally reading through those notes. Even though I was motivated it was very difficult for me to stay alert and alive in such a setting. The professor was well known in his field and had published, but he was devoid of any ability to teach. He was in stark contract to my statistics professor. In a university setting students for the most part teach themselves, but in primary and secondary schools teachers have to literally teach, which means they have to engage the interest of their students. When you have 28 students in your classroom this is not an easy task.

In American high schools sports coaches are more important than teachers, or at least it seems that way. Teachers can be lousy, their students can do poorly on exams, but they hardly ever get fired, but woe to the coach whose team has a losing season. When I was introduced to my son's math teacher at Saucon I was told that 'he is the baseball coach you know' as if this made him a better math teacher. Every American High School, whether in Pennsylvania, Texas, or Alabama, have basketball courts and lighted football stadiums with seating. Games are the high light of the school week, and parents who would never think of entering a classroom will flock to the games. At American universities it is common for the coaches to be paid more, much more, that the university President. At the University of Alabama the head football coach is paid $4 million a year. Can you imagine the head of the physics department being paid that kind of salary?

Coaches are people who not only know their game and how to play it, but above and beyond that they know how to mold a bunch of kids into a winning team. At the university level of course they have the advantage of being able to recruit nationwide, but on the other hand if they lose, their tenure is brief (tenure does not apply to coaches!). At the high school level, although they have to choose their players from the kids in the school, they are also expected to win. A friend of mine who was a long term football coach at a local high school enjoyed many years of success, but suddenly, for whatever reason, his teams started losing. He survived a couple of years and was then unceremoniously promoted out and replaced. He suddenly felt a failure.

In many ways a teacher needs to be a coach. A good coach demands practice, demands attendance, demands good behavior, demands effort, and gets it. Of course the kids want to be on the team, and the coach has the ability to threaten them with dismissal if they do not do what he wants, whereas a teacher lacks this threat, except to a very small degree. If kids misbehave in school they can be sent to in school detention or some similar program, but this only works if the kid wants to be in school. The kids who misbehave are usually the ones who do not want to be in school and are only too happy to get out.

The Teacher as Disciplinarian

The life of a teacher is much pleasanter if the students are respectful and well behaved but as is well established this is frequently not the case, especially in inner city schools. The teacher therefore has to learn how to manage a classroom, and although some of this can be taught from a book, I think, as I have already said, that the best place to learn how to do it is in an actual classroom. Every real classroom starts off by being a contest between the one (the teacher) and the many (25 students). It is important that the teacher asserts him or herself from the beginning. Just as students who want to succeed have to establish their reputation so teachers who want to succeed have to establish their reputations, and the earlier the better.

In Texas there were teachers who had excellent classroom management skills, and teachers who did not. Once a teacher has a certain reputation, it is very difficult to change, as incoming students know what to expect and how to behave. The chances of a student learning anything if the classroom is chaotic are slim, there is simply too much noise, buzz, and confusion.

When I first came to the United States I was hired by the College of New Jersey to run one of their men's dormitories. Apparently it was out of control and the administration thought that my background in delinquency might be useful! My predecessor (who in typical college fashion was not fired but simply transferred to a less onerous job) was a very weak man who wanted everyone to like him, a fatal error if you want to control and manage people. I was told that students were drinking, having girls in their rooms, firing guns, and so on. It took me one day to impose my authority. I was urinating in the public restroom and a tall young man came in and said "Oh Hi David, you must be the new dorm director." I replied "Yes I am, but I would like you to call me Mr. Austin unless I tell you differently." That was all it basically took. The word got around that I was not to be messed with, and everybody settled down to a peaceful and productive year. When I arrived in Naples to work at the Casa it took me longer to assert my authority. I knew no Italian when I arrived, I was a foreigner, and I did not understand the culture. The staff simply hit the kids if they did not obey, but I did not wish to do that even though I realized that that was what they were used to. It took me about six weeks of unremitting effort, but one day the kids accepted me and from that day forward my slightest wish was followed without a problem, and I could afford to relax. The classroom can be a battlefield, and a teacher needs to make sure that she or he is the victor, not the students.

Performance Evaluation

Whenever I lie back in the dentist's chair I wonder whether the man hovering over me graduated with an A or a C average. I am encouraged by the thought that the training program for dentists is very rigorous, or at least so I am told. Moreover most dentists are solo practitioners, and their salary depends on their ability to attract customers. How do I find a good dentist when I go to a new town? I ask people who have already used him or her. If he does not have a good reputation as established by this survey, I simply do not use him – there is always a choice. When I move to a new town with my children I typically have to accept the school that is there (unless I choose a private school and am willing to pay for it), and within that school I have to accept whatever teachers work there. I can of course ask other parents what the various teachers are like, but these opinions are likely to be varied, and in any case if I ask that my child be transferred I will be asked why, and if all I have to base my opinion on is other peoples' opinions, I am not going to get very far. Principals do not want to face the fact that some of their teachers are better than others, so they choose to ignore the whole issue and hope that it does not raise its ugly head. As I have said, if sports teams start losing, the coach is blamed, but if students fail to pass exams, the students are blamed. It would be a much simpler process if there were some form of objective data to which a parent could refer. To me the fact that someone has a degree is certainly important but what I really want to know is whether he can teach my children.

League tables in England have created a measure of school performance, and in areas where there are multiple schools parents have some choice, and of course they all want to get their children into the higher performing schools. This can result in high emotion as parents fail to get their child into the 'best' school. There is little in the way of information about the teachers however.

The issue of teacher performance measurement has been around for a long time, and to date has never been established as a routine process. Years ago, when I was teaching at Temple University, the administration established a program whereby the students evaluated their professors. The results were published. Needless to say many tenured professors were viewed by their students as very poor teachers. Everyone – except the tenured professors – had a good laugh, the faculty union declared the survey worthless and unscientific, the administration buckled, and the whole idea vanished.

It goes without saying that no one likes to be evaluated, but it needs to be remembered that the students are the consumers of the educational system, not the teachers. No one to my knowledge has argued that students should not be evaluated; how else can you measure whether they have learned anything. Teachers measure students all the time, whether formally or informally. But when the same scores that are used to evaluate students are turned around and used to evaluate teachers there is widespread resistance. Teachers do not want to be responsible for the success or failure of their students. This is curious when you think about it. If they are not responsible for their students learning, what are they responsible for, and how can one ascertain whether students have learned anything except by examining them?

All activities should be measured by their outcomes, and education should be no exception. The new Secretary for Education in England, Ed Balls, is proposing to have teachers re-licensed every five years, a process which will be administered by their principals. Teachers who fail this process will automatically be ineligible to teach, although there will of course be an appeals process. It remains to be seen whether this will be implemented. Mr. Balls will probably be out of office in one year. Unions and teachers have a far longer shelf life than Education Secretaries.

Teacher Unions

I have always felt that unions have no place in human services. Unions' main weapon is the strike, and I think it unethical for anyone whose work consists in assisting other human beings in some way to walk off the job. I do not view someone who signs over their right to negotiate their benefits and salary to some third party as a professional, and teachers want to be viewed as professional.

Teacher Unions have always fought against student progress as a measurement of teacher competence. Recently in New York City Randi Weingarten, the President of the United Federation of Teachers, was quoted as saying she had grave reservations about student progress to measure teacher quality. It is one thing for unions to fight for improved wages, but quite another for them to resist objective evaluation.

In my many years as a boss I fought unionization tooth and nail. Why? I did not want an external company (the Union) telling me how to do my job. When I helped develop an institution for the mentally retarded within Temple University I was told by the administration that they officially welcomed unionization. When I asked Temple's head of labor relations why, he said it was much simpler across the university if everyone was unionized, and he reckoned that he could always produce contracts which were workable and to the benefit of the university as a whole. While I understood that it made life simpler for him, I doubt that it was to the benefit of the university as a whole. When I helped develop the program the workers under me were not initially unionized of course, so there had to be a process of unionization. The union did what they often do. They put out leaflets which proclaimed all the benefits that staff would incur as a result of voting for the union. Most of the claims were totally untrue, but I was not allowed to say so. The union spread rumors about the sexual activities of various administrators including myself, which once again we were not allowed to deny. There was a certain amount of tire slashing and other forms of property destruction. Needless to say the union was quickly voted in, whereupon I had to adhere to the union contract. It meant among other things that it became very difficult to fire staff.

The item in any contract that I have the most difficulty with apart from the right to strike is tenure. All union contracts attempt to establish tenure as early as possible, whereupon it becomes almost impossible to fire someone. The result is that if you wish to get rid of a staff person you have do it very early on. I would abolish tenure throughout the education system, from kindergarten to graduate school. Competent teachers do not need it – their jobs are safe. The teachers who need it are the incompetent. Furthermore unions fight all attempts to distinguish between average employees and superior employees, and various forms of merit pay. Finally the chief weapon of unions is the strike, and as I have said I object to people who work with people who would walk off the job because their union told them to.

There was an interesting story recently by Karen Matthews in the Associated Press. It appears that 700 New York City teachers are being paid a full salary to sit around and do nothing. These are teachers who have been accused of offences ranging from insubordination to sexual misconduct, and are waiting for formal hearings. They sit in so-called 'rubber rooms' which have been specifically set up for this purpose, and put in their hours doing whatever they want to do, except teach. The city Department of Education estimates the cost at $65 million a year. In Los Angeles there are 178 teachers languishing in this limbo state. In other districts teachers are simply sent home. According to the article, waiting for the process of hearings to resolve their status can take months, and sometimes years. This is because there are only 23 arbitrators, and they only work five days a month. Administrators say that these teachers were fired for cause; teachers of course say that they were fired for petty stuff or simply because someone did not like them. It is a typical bureaucratic nightmare.

Unions have succeeded in raising employees' pay, but at what cost? A good argument can be made that the current problems that the American car industry is having is attributable in part to the very expensive contracts which the unions managed to obtain for their workers, and which resulted in American companies being handicapped in their competition with companies from Germany, Japan, and Korea. Part of the blame of course rests with the bosses of General Motors and Chrysler who capitulated again and again to union demands when faced with strikes. The end result is that Chrysler has been sold, General

Motors has been downsized and taken over by the government, and thousands of union employees have lost their jobs. The remaining employees of course still have their union, and I have no doubt that this will continue to be a problem as General Motors and Chrysler try to be reborn.

In my opinion unions do not care about the health of the companies where their members work, they care only about the wages and working conditions of the workers. The result is that managers are constrained in what they do unless they are willing to play hardball. In a field where the relationship between workers and managers is meant to be cordial this I think is counterproductive.

Obama has announced a 'Race to the Top' initiative. He is throwing in 4.5 billion dollars of federal money in an attempt to get the States and the schools to do what he wants them to do, which is to change, to measure teacher competence, to be open to competition, and to raise the bar academically, partly through adopting common academic standards across the nation. 4.5 billion sounds like a lot, but the stimulus bill already contained 100 billion for education, and the federal government in America and the national government in England have been throwing money at the schools for many decades with very limited results in terms of student progress in reading and math and science. A study which looked at education funding in various countries from 1995-2003 found no relationship between education spending and math scores.

Obama is basically saying to the States, if you do what I want you to do, then I will give you money. A large obstacle is the union. While Obama was preaching his message of change and competition, the union in Washington DC, one of the worst school systems in the country, succeeding in closing a popular school voucher program, even though it was seemingly improving test scores for low income minorities. Unions are opposed to student choice, however defined, and are opposed to evaluating teachers based on student performance, even though this is surely what they are meant to be doing.

Detroit is an example of a school system going nowhere. Only 25% of the students graduate on time. Only 16% of 11th graders scored proficient in math – statewide 49% did. Reading and science scores are equally poor. The cost per student is $1700 more than the state average. The system is bankrupt, and losing students. It is the home of General Motors. An attempt to reduce costs by reducing teacher salaries was met with an illegal strike, which was nevertheless successful. More people are beginning to recognize that the only solution is formal bankruptcy, sidelining the union, and making a fresh start.

Randi Weingarten the head of the union, claims that any real educator can know within five minutes of walking into a classroom if a teacher is effective. She does not say how this is in fact done. As Professor Kane of Harvard states, it is hard to know who is going to be an effective classroom teacher until they are actually in the classroom, but that few school districts spend much time trying to assess new teachers, which is when they need help the most. I once again reiterate that teacher education should take place in the school classroom and not in college.

Chapter Four

What Do Schools Bring to Education?

"Education has produced a vast population able to read but unable to distinguish what is worth reading.." G.M. Trevelyan

Teachers work in buildings called schools which have not changed in one hundred years. They essentially consist of a number of boxes called classrooms, together with a number of ancillary rooms. If the school is in America it will have at least one basketball court and a large stadium for football. Depending on the size of the school and the wealth of the neighborhood there may an indoor swimming pool, and an impressive theater. The school is surrounded by playing fields and, in America, huge parking lots. Needless to say schools serving good areas tend to be nicer and have better results than schools serving poor areas, especially schools serving the inner cities. There have been occasional attempts to change the format of school buildings, but with little success. Recently teachers in England asked to go back to individual classrooms after an experiment with an open structure, which they said interfered with learning.

Schools also have an administration, which consists in one or more principals/headmasters, a fiscal office, ancillary staff, and a superintendent/head who is responsible for a district/collection of schools. They not only deal with the various office functions, but they direct the work of the teachers.

Finally there are School Boards of one kind or another, who are elected by the local community and are meant to represent it. The School Board hires and evaluates the superintendent/headmaster, probably its most important task.

There is no doubt in my mind that schools are the most important organizational part of the educational jigsaw, and that the most important person in the school is the Headmaster/Principal/Superintendent. To a large extent the question of whether an individual student will obtain the best education is dependent on the school he attends, and in turn the quality of the school depends very much on the person who runs that school, especially when the school has students who have been doing poorly and who come from impoverished backgrounds. While generally speaking the best schools are in the best neighborhoods, there are examples of poor schools that have been turned around by a competent Head. It does seem to be possible, and in both England and America the hope of turning around the low quality education received by the lower classes rests largely on that assumption. However it takes a remarkable person to change a poor school into a good one. There are examples.

For instance there is Norview High School in Virginia. Historically the school had met the State's passing rate of 70% in only one subject, reading. Black students, who make up 70% of the students, lagged behind their white peers by as much as 40 percent. Under the leadership of a new Superintendent, the school adopted a new approach to learning, emphasizing serious test preparation, and raising expectations for both teachers and students. Success in State tests and the SAT were widely publicized. There was some pain, and some teachers left, but the result was that scores improved across the school, and students took pride in their academic achievement.

The problem is finding enough inspirational leaders who can turn failing schools around.

School Quality

Schools vary enormously in quality as measured by student performance. There is a whole industry in both America and England which ranks schools on a variety of measures, typically by student outcomes on objective exams of one kind or another. What these rankings show is that private schools do better than public schools on the average; that schools in good locations do better than schools in poor locations, and that schools who admit good students do better than schools who admit poor students. All of this is rather common-sensical and predictable. Take one recent English study. The Sutton Trust tracked 550,000 students who took the national SAT exam in 2001 and tracked them through high school until they took their final exams (GCSE's) six years later. Schools were categorized according to the number of students eligible for free meals because of family poverty level. What the study showed was that students who were of similar ability in 2001 differed significantly six years later. Students who attended poverty schools did much worse than students who attended non-poverty schools. It was suggested that this was because of poor pupil behavior, mediocre teaching, and a greater emphasis on vocational courses. In America, in California, more than 1,000 schools out of 9,500 are branded chronic failures. In 2007 in Abraham Lincoln High School only 7 percent of the students could do grade-level math or English, while at Woodrow Wilson High only 4 percent could. In America only 70 percent of students nationally graduate from high school. In New York City less than 50 percent of the students were graduating on time. In Detroit it was 24.9 percent! Needless to say the worst schools tend to be in the worst locations, have the worst students, the worst buildings, the lowest budgets, and the worst teachers, and the worst administrators.

In 2009 English test results showed that 25% of primary school students could not read or write fluently, nor do basic arithmetic. What this means is that they cannot add, subtract, multiply, or divide in their heads, and they cannot write extended sentences using commas. As primary school education is the foundation for all that comes afterwards, this means that many children enter high school without the basic skills necessary to success. It immediately makes the high school a remedial institution for many of its students.

Obviously if all students are to enjoy a quality education, all schools have to be quality schools, within a narrow range. I assume there is some variation between medical schools and more between law schools, but on the whole one can assume that this range is fairly narrow and that a graduate of any of them has a reasonable level of competence. But these are graduate professional schools, and the poor students never get that far. One can make no such assumption about state primary and secondary schools, nor about high schools, nor about many colleges for that matter. There is enormous variation, and therefore an enormous difference between the quality of education experienced by a student in one school as opposed to another. Recently some law students were meeting with Justice Scalia and one of them asked him how someone could become a clerk to a Supreme Court Justice. Only by being a graduate of Yale or Harvard Law School he answered.

The Principal/Headmaster

But there is hope, and that hope seems to rest on finding a person to lead a failing school who can turn it around. In May 2008 there was a story in the New York Times about a man called George Leonard, principal of Bedford Academy High School in Bedford-Stuyvesant, Brooklyn. 63 percent of his students qualify for a free lunch, a majority are being raised by single mothers, and many by someone other than a parent. They resemble the students in Texas, except that there are more of them. 95 percent of his students graduate, and almost all of them go on to college of one kind or another. How does he do it?

'I wanted to prove that no matter what the competency, a child could still be successful,' he said. In the eighties he had taken a group of typical elementary school children and decided that he could teach them to pass the Regents' Exam in biology, an exam normally given in the ninth grade. He succeeded. He did it by imposing clear demands on the students. Now at Bedford he insists that all entering students spend their Saturday mornings in prep classes the summer before they are admitted. He tells them that they cannot come to his school unless they go through this program. This is not in fact true – it is a Leonard mandate, and could not be enforced. Once the student enrolls, if he finds they are struggling academically, he requires them to attend Saturday study sessions which run from 9 in the morning to 9 at night! He assigns the most experienced teachers to the students who are having the greatest problems. He continuously evaluates teachers, and if they do not produce results, he lets them go. He also continuously evaluates whether students are making the desired progress. 'Quiz them to death' he says. Finally he demands that the students' parents or surrogates support what he is trying to do. He does not believe in homework, but he has no time for parents who complain. Parents also need to believe in their kids, is the way he frames it.

There are a number of similar examples of educator leaders turning failing schools around. An English example is William Atkinson. He emigrated with his family from Jamaica when he was 7. He is now head of Phoenix High School in London. About two thirds of the students have learning difficulties, a tenth are refugees or asylum seekers, and about half speak English as a second language. The area is the seventh poorest in the country. Yet the exam results are around the national average which, given the starting point, is remarkable. Before Atkinson arrived it was regarded as a hopeless school. Students were throwing furniture out of the windows, setting fires to the buildings, and plastering graffiti on every available surface. There had been five heads and two acting heads in two years. When the local education authority which ran the school sought him out he told them he would take the job, but only if they promised not to interfere with what he needed to do. On arrival he demanded that the teachers produce detailed lesson plans for every lesson, and that senior staff observe lessons. The teachers threatened to walk out but on arbitration he got his way. Some teachers left, but that was fine. As he said, what he found was some teachers who were very good, but they were such a small number that they had a limited effect; a large number of very ordinary teachers; and another large number of temporary and supply teachers. He made it his business to find and hire outstanding teachers.

Ofsted in England agrees absolutely that the solution to bad schools is to fire bad heads and hire good ones. Give them the money and leave them alone. If they do not work out, fire them and find another one. It sounds simple, but the problem is finding the people. Being a headmaster or principal is far from an easy task, and has become more difficult over the years. Over a thousand retire or quit every year. The result is that in 2008 in England hundreds of schools were left without a head. Twenty percent of 1,930 schools where heads had left that year had been unable to find a replacement. The National Association of Head Teachers gives three reasons for the lack of leadership recruits: the administrative burdens, the public naming of schools experiencing difficulty, and curiously enough the tendency to avoid outstanding schools because if you start at the top the only way in league tables is down! As an example of an administrative burden there is a proposed rule, now working its way through Parliament, which would ban the custom of teachers putting examples of student work up on walls, a rule which is designed to reduce the amount of non-teaching work required of teachers!

The problem does not seem to be as severe in America, at least at this time, but the challenges are similar. In a study of school superintendents, who manage school districts containing multiple schools, the following problems were listed:

Local politics frequently intruded into district policy making.

Demands from different constituencies often conflict with each other.

Federal and State mandates hamstring decision making.

State standards, accountability, and assessments create overwhelming pressure.

Boards micromanage the district and the superintendent.

Boards are unfocused.

Union contracts are rigid and prevent the implementation of some needed reforms.

Districts would like to respond to the public's wishes, but public demands frequently change.

Central offices are overly bureaucratic and resist change.

Board turnover is frequent and makes it hard to maintain support for district initiatives.

What then does one look for in a Head/Principal? Recently in America a coalition of education groups published the Educational Leadership Policy Standards. At the same time the National Association of Elementary School Principals came up with their set. These stated that effective leaders of learning communities (!) would:

Lead schools in a way that places student and adult learning at the center.

Set high expectations for the academic, social, emotional, and physical development of all students.

Demand content and instruction that ensure student achievement of agreed-on standards.

Foster a culture of continuous learning for adults tied to student learning and other school goals.

Manage data and knowledge to inform decisions and measure progress of student, adult, and school performance.

Actively engage the community to establish shared responsibility for student performance and development.

These standards sound fine and dandy. The question of course is how to implement them, and what they leave out.

The University of Virginia pioneered an interesting program whereby turnaround specialists were sent into failing schools. The program was developed through a collaboration between the University's Colleges of Education and Business. Professor Duke published some of the things that had been learned as the program was developed.

1. There is no substitute for leadership. Someone has to take charge, and this someone has to typically come from outside. The University tried to find examples where existing staff in failing schools had organized themselves to turn things around, but had been unable to find any. It is very difficult to change things from the inside because of the relationships that exist, the habitual way things have always been done, and the prevalence of denial that anything is wrong. To take General Motors as an example, for years commentators had been urging radical action, but the company had chugged along as usual. While the last CEO was cheerleading and saying how wonderful the company was, it was losing market share every year. The same thing happened at IBM when it was in trouble. The CEO in place was floundering and could not bring himself to do what was necessary, and it was not until the company brought in Louis Gerstner from outside that the necessary decisions were made. Schools are even more difficult to

change than businesses, given the innate conservatism of education at all levels, and the multiple parties that are involved in any decision making, including boards, parents, communities, politicians, teachers, district offices, and so on. The fact is that leaders have to be nasty on occasion, and have to be ruthless on occasion, and most people hate being either of those things. Inevitably if a school is failing there are teachers who are incompetent, and who therefore have to be removed, even though they may have been in place for years. No one likes doing this, but it has to be done if things are to change

2. If teachers are to be fired then it is necessary not only to be able to identify incompetent teachers, but also to have a record of attempted interventions and their results – the process needs to be fair. Teachers need to be clear about their job expectations and need to be evaluated annually, and more often when they are new. When my wife was hired by the Texas school to run a program for students who were demonstrating behavioral problems, she was neither given a job description, not was she evaluated once during the two year she held the position. She was essentially left to her own devices. She was not even sure which of the administrators was her supervisor as her program served the whole school. My sense at the school was that no one was ever evaluated. At raise time everyone was simply given the same raise (except for the administrators of course) so that no teachers were identified as being better than any others. The teachers who taught the core subjects were in fact very good, I think, but this was not true of some of those responsible for teaching other subjects. The fact is that the whole question of whether to get rid of an incompetent teacher was based not so much on whether they harmed their students, but on other factors. One factor was the whole problem of hiring a replacement when you are running a small school in a poor rural area miles from anywhere. Then again spouses were often both hired which meant of course that firing one of them would

have implications for the other. All three administrators had wives who were hired on the teaching staff and were therefore theoretically supervised by their husbands. If both spouses were competent, and occupied equivalent positions, it made sense. On the other hand spouses sometimes seemed to be hired simply because of their relationship. Finally terminations upset people. They are politically incorrect. In the six years we spent in Texas, only two teachers were fired, and both were from out of the area, so lacked community support and interest. On the other hand one of the staff whom everyone agreed was incompetent appeared to be immoveable. She had lived in the community for years, and had been on the staff for years, and no one wanted to upset anyone!

3. The leader needs to stay around to make sure that any changes are thoroughly implemented and monitored and adjusted as needed. There is no such thing as a short term fix. In my six years in Texas there were three superintendents, three high school principals, and two elementary school principals, the second of whom is leaving next year. It is difficult to operate an outstanding school if there is constant change at the top. New people bring different personalities, and different ideas, and are the new boys on the block compared to their faculty, some of whom may have been around for years. Another problem is that, given the structure of the system, the former administrator leaves before the new one comes on board. The tendency is to leave well alone unless there are significant problems. The new person looks around, and adjusts to the situation.

The major problem of course is that there are thousands of failing schools, and not nearly enough charismatic and energetic and knowledgeable leaders who can turn things around. Being an outstanding teacher does not lead to being an outstanding administrator. While Colonel Stevens was alive and running the school Chelmsford Hall was a wonderful place which achieved great things. He had three sons. One of them was being groomed to take over and did so when the Colonel retired. He used to visit the school when I was there and he was one of those people born to work with children. I can remember him vividly across the years even though his visits were brief. Unfortunately he died shortly after taking over. The other son had to move into the gap and I will always wonder what might have happened to the Hall had that untimely death not intervened. The other son ran the school for many years, but he was not the same man as his brother or father. When in turn he came to retirement there was no one to take over the school, it was too small to attract a buyer, so it closed. It had a life of 72 years. In a sense it was always too small to compete, and eventually lost out to bigger and better capitalized rival schools. I have a vision of Colonel Stevens turning over in his grave.

My daughter currently attends a small private school in Alabama. It is as far as I can make out, broke. There is a competing school in a neighboring town which has succeeded in siphoning off students because it offers a much better sports program – always an important issue in America – and a greater variety of programs in general, simply because of size. Parents who live in our small town pay to have their children bussed there. The question is, how can my daughter's school reverse that flow? One idea that is being implemented is to have seniors take courses for credit at a local college This is something that the other school does not presently offer. Public schools though do offer such courses. The school in Texas for instance offered dual credit (as they were called) starting in a student's junior year, so that by the time a student graduated he or she could amass quite a few credits, which would then count towards a degree, depending on the college he attended. This raises another question.

The main difference between private and public schools is not so much the programs they offer, but the students they admit. In many ways public schools, especially in America, have facilities which are very impressive, especially in regard to sports, but also in academic areas. At the top of the league tables in England there are a number of private schools, but there are also a number of public schools. Tonbridge for instance placed 40 in the most recent tables, and in first place was a state school, which was located in a very expensive town just outside of London. Saucon had brand new buildings, multiple gymnasiums, an indoor swimming pool, a theater, and a football stadium, to mention the most obvious. Tonbridge has just built an indoor swimming pool, but if you want to watch football or cricket you have to stand on your own two feet on the grass surrounding the field. In order to justify its enormous fees places like Tonbridge have to produce academically. State schools simply have to be.

When I talk about failing schools then, I am talking about failing students. The students that present challenges to the educational system are largely students who come from poor backgrounds, with deficient (in this context) cultures, made even more problematic by issues of race and language and religion. The question is, how do you change those students?

Obama's new Secretary of Education, Arne Duncan, is planning to tackle the problem head-on by closing failing schools, and re-opening them with new principals and new staff. Federal data shows that there are some 6,000 failing schools in America, and that little has been done to correct them, largely because of lethargy on the part of State and local officials. Mr. Duncan has no authority to close schools directly, and will have to convince the local power structure that it is the right thing to do. He is planning on closing 250 schools in 2010, and 1000 schools every year thereafter.

When he ran the Chicago school system Mr. Duncan closed down a dozen schools despite intense opposition. Some seem to have been successful, some not. All required laying off hundreds of teachers with no guarantee that they would be re-hired, and of course the replacement of the administration. But it is clear that something drastic has to be done if anything is to change. The process also costs of lot of money, but Obama has already given him the necessary billions. It will be fascinating to see how this initiative unfolds.

Money

Schools need to operate like good businesses. They need to stay within their budgets, and make sensible financial decisions. My impression is that public schools have plenty of money and if they get into trouble it is more because of poor management than lack of funds.

Shortly before we arrived in Texas the school was broke. It had spent more than its revenues. The State came in and threatened to take it over. The problem was that the superintendent had spent money that he did not have. Moreover the Board made no attempt to supervise him – they were not even getting monthly financial statements. The superintendent was fired, and his replacements started rectifying the situation. By the time we left the school was in excellent financial shape and the superintendent (who was the third person in the position after the episode) was on top of things. Not only did the school have a positive fund balance, but a new computer lab had been built, new electrical and air-conditioning and heating systems put in, a new floor laid in the elementary gym, and the athletic track renovated. Meanwhile the school census was declining as young families were not moving into the area, but this did not seem to be a fiscal problem.

The declining census was creating a problem in football however. The lack of students meant that the school did not have enough footballers, and started to lose all of their games. As I have said, football is far more important than academics in most American schools, and is something which communities focus on. It is possible that in the future this will have a domino effect as families with young male children will not move into the area. State schools can function even if they are very small, but the pressure to merge with other small schools in the area will doubtless increase.

The school in Alabama is experiencing all the problems of a small private school. It is dependent on parent fees, and therefore is greatly affected by fluctuations in census. Furthermore, while the school in Texas has no competition for students, the school in Alabama is threatened by that neighboring school which is a bus ride away. Fees in both schools are comparable. The other school charges for the bus ride, but it seems that the school's better athletic programs outweigh this factor. The town is not increasing in population, so that it is difficult to see where new students are going to come from. There is a local public school of course, which is almost entirely black and poor, so it is highly unlikely that the school will be able to attract these students.

The current census at the school is 85, which is where Chelmsford Hall was. Without additional sources of funds this does not seem to be a critical mass. The school would like to have 135 students, but where are they to come from? As I noted, they have started a program with the local College which will enable senior students to earn college credit which seems to be innovative in this area, but they do not offer advanced placement courses which are common in most States, and which can be pursued on the internet (Texas offered dual credit classes starting in the junior year, and AP courses were also available). Chelmsford Hall tried offering programs for students with learning disabilities, programs for students from abroad, and started admitting girls, and all of these initiatives helped for a while, but in the long run were not enough. If you are a small private school you have to be able to compete – it is the nature of the beast – and you have to compete both academically and on the playing field – that is what parents want. To do this you have to be a certain size. You also have to have enough parents willing to pay the fees. In the current economic recession, for instance, many smaller less prestigious private schools in England are having to merge with more stable rivals, or shut down completely, which is what happened with Chelmsford Hall.

Saucon Valley has the best of all worlds. Not only is it a public school but it is located in an area which is increasing in population, and moreover increasing with a wealthy population. It is large, 2500 students, and had few problems that I could see. Although there were private schools in the area few parents saw any reason to send their children there. Tonbridge, after experiencing some problems during the war years, has steadily increased in renown and size, and is now able to charge some of the highest fees in the country, and obtain them without a problem because of its reputation. But the state schools in Tonbridge are also excellent, and it will be interesting to see whether parents will continue to believe that the high fees are worth it.

Chapter Five

What Does the Bureaucracy Bring to Education?

I will define the bureaucracy as everything outside the school district. Both England and America have State Departments of Education, and Ministers in charge of them. In recent years the bureaucracies in both countries have steadily increased, as government bureaucracies always seem to do. Whereas in the early days of education schools had a great deal of leeway in what they taught students, now this is typically defined by the State; in the early days teachers were people who wanted to teach and had some ability to do that; now the qualifications and role of the teacher are increasingly defined by the State; in the early days teachers determined which students had been successfully taught, now the definition of success is increasingly defined by the State. Like all government entities, departments of education grow from year to year, thinking up new ways of influencing things, which in turn require more and more staff to make sure that this influence is working, or to change things if it is not working. The bureaucracy views their role as supporting education; schools view the bureaucracy as an unnecessary burden. The issue is further confounded in America by the power of individual States' rights, and the constant tension between the Federal government and the 50 states, a tension which is much stronger than the tension between London and the Counties in England. The first problem then is the problem of control.

Control

As should be obvious by now I think that schools can only be outstanding if the boss is a leader who is capable of doing the job and who has enough degrees of freedom to do what he/she needs to do. In other words, he or she has to have power and a substantial amount of freedom. One of the major issues in education and other fields is that if government funds you, it also wants to control you. It seems to me reasonable that this should be so, but only up to a point. To some extent whoever pays you always controls you. Even in the business world, businesses have to respond to their consumers or else they will be quickly out of business. The real question is the extent of the control within that framework.

I spent most of my life working in what can broadly be defined as human services. My first experience was at the Casa dello Scugnizzo in Naples, Italy. The Casa had been created by an Italian priest called Mario Borrelli. After the war Naples and other Italian cities were in poor shape, and one of the outcomes was the number of children who lived on the streets, using their wits to forage a living. Borrelli obtained an old abandoned church in one of the poorer districts, took off his priestly attire, and went on the streets himself. As he said, the children would never trust him unless they got to know him first. Gradually he befriended them and persuaded a number to come and live in the church. He scraped together money from wherever he could, with some support from the church, some from the city, and some from the state. In 1957 Morris West wrote a book about him and he suddenly became famous. Various fund raising groups were set up in England and other places, and life became a little easier.

I arrived there in September 1960. I had been searching for something worthwhile to do, and a friend, an English monk, suggested that I go to help in any way that I could. The old church was in a little square at the end of a narrow road, surrounded by tenements. Its façade bore some traces of its former glory. Borrelli had an office in front above the main entrance. Within the main building there were a couple of rooms for the smallest boys, who were aged six and up. There was also a kitchen and a shower room. Down the corridor one came to a courtyard at the back, where there were two sheds with corrugated metal roofs, one the dining room, and one a dormitory.

Surrounding the courtyard were more tenements whose inhabitants could look down on us. On one side it opened to a junk yard, which Borrelli operated to raise some money, and which supplied wood for the kitchen.

There were some 30 boys, aged between 6 and 14. I did not know what to expect. I knew little Italian, and in any case I had to learn Neapolitan, which was the dialect that all the boys spoke. Borrelli gave me a small bedroom up near the top of the dome. Initially I helped out with office work, but I ate with the boys, and in the evenings played soccer with them in the dusty courtyard. There were a couple of young men who acted as 'professori' and were in charge of the boys. There was a secretary and a book-keeper and a porter, and up near my bedroom two ladies spent their days patching old clothing so that the boys would have something to wear. There was also a cook.

One of Borrelli's major problems was finding professori who were reliable. They tended to come for a while, and then disappear as soon as they found a better paying job. They varied in their ability to manage the boys, and they also varied in their attitude. After I had been there sixteen weeks Borrelli put me in charge.

In many ways it was the best work I have ever had. The boys themselves, once they trusted you, were delightful. They were at the Casa because, for one reason or another, their parents were unable or did not wish to look after them. They were under no obligation to stay if they did not wish to, and every now and again one of them would take off, but a couple of days later would come back. We dressed them as well as we could, and fed them as well as we could. They all went to school for half a day, which was the normal thing in Italy at the time. The care we gave them was basic: feed them, clothe them, give them some education, give them a bed to sleep in, protect them from harm, and hope to give them a future. As the boys entered their teens they went down to another house, which was on top of the roof of the Oratory opposite the cathedral, and were given vocational training.

I stayed there three years until I decided it was time I earned some money. I found a job as Deputy Superintendent of Hutton Poplars Childrens' Home. Hutton was an institution located in Essex, just outside of London, and served children and adolescents who were either in need of care or who had run foul of the law. There were some

300 children, babies through teenagers, of both sexes. They lived in one of a number of houses, each with about 28 beds, organized around a village green. There was an indoor heated swimming pool, a chapel, and a large assembly room. Some of the children only stayed there short-term, but many spent years there.

The difference between the Casa and Hutton was dramatic. At the Casa Borrelli was in charge, and could essentially operate how he saw fit. There were no rules except his; no regulations except his; no inspectors, no case managers, no social workers, no files on the children. At Hutton, because it was state funded, there were reams of regulations, frequent visits by state inspectors, a contract psychiatrist, lots of case managers and social workers, and forms for everything. I spent hours in meetings which were held in order to fill up the files with information which frequently just lay there until the next meeting. The children were for the most part just as nice as the ones in Naples, but they had more anger in them. Hutton was in the suburbs so the children had been uprooted from their familiar surroundings and dropped into this middle class world. They could not leave if they wished to. If they ran away, they were brought back, or placed in a closed facility. They ached to get back to their familiar surroundings, in the slums of London. The children in Naples were still in their familiar surroundings, and if they went out of the front door they felt at home, and if they wanted to come back, they could. They were free: the children in Hutton were essentially prisoners.

On the other hand, Hutton had plenty of money. One of my most vivid memories was the time at the end of the fiscal year when the Superintendent urged everyone to go on a spending spree in order to make sure the entire budget was exhausted. If it was not, then the following year's budget would be based on what was spent, not on what was approved. Heaven forbid that should happen. Later on I found that this was a common process in state funded enterprises of all kinds, both in England and America.

The Casa was a free-standing enterprise, dependent on the energy and intelligence of one person. Obviously Borrelli worked within certain constraints. He had less money to spend than the Superintendent of Hutton, but on the other hand, what he had he could spend as he chose. Hutton had to produce all kinds of reports, Borrelli did not.

The Superintendent had to report to the London County Council, for which he worked. He also had a Board of Directors, made up of various politicians. Borrelli had none of these things. The Superintendent had to work within an established London County Council framework which essentially configured most of what he did. He was very sensitive to anything that might be viewed as a negative comment on his administration. He was much more interested in keeping on the right side of his political bosses than on improving the lives of the children in his care.

Eventually Hutton closed when the prevailing opinion determined that institutions were bad things, but this decision was totally out of the Superintendent's hands. Borrelli had the problem of raising enough money to operate, but when he decided to close the residential service and replace it with an array of social services to the local community, it was his decision. The Superintendent had to spend energy making sure he was pleasing his boss and Board. Borrelli was his own boss.

The Superintendent took over an existing program and ran it well or poorly but did not change it. When he retired someone else took over. Borrelli created a brand new program, was in charge of it for his lifetime, and elected his successor. The program would not have existed without him.

I think that if a failing school is to be changed, then a new boss has to be brought in, he has to be given the power and the authority to do whatever needs to be done, and then he needs to be left alone to do it. He needs to feel that it is his program, his responsibility. If he succeeds he should be rewarded; if he fails he should be fired.

Private schools likeTonbridge, Chelmsford Hall, Swain, and the school in Alabama all benefit from being more or less independent. They are or were all largely independent of government money and therefore independent to a significant degree from government interference. They are not totally free. They have to prepare students for examinations like everyone else. They have state inspections at various points, but nowhere near the burden experienced by state schools. The fact that the Hall eventually closed, and that the school in Alabama is experiencing problems simply underlines the fact that more degrees of freedom also add up to more degrees of risk – it goes with the territory.

When I started LifePath I was grateful. I had discovered that I could not work for other people, and therefore needed to be Boss. LifePath allowed me to be that for 22 years. I created a large organization from scratch. To do it I needed lots of State money, and with the money came all kinds of regulations and rules and constraints, so what I had to do was learn how to obey the rules while at the same time doing what I needed to do. I took all kinds of risks as I went along because you can achieve nothing unless you take risks, but they were risks that were thought through, and moreover the risks were taken to benefit LifePath and the people it serves. I was driven by the desire to serve as many people as I could and to serve them as well as I could. I had a Board of Directors, which I sometimes regretted, but they were a good Board, and most of the time very supportive. When I retired, LifePath was a strong organization with a healthy fund balance a wonderful staff, and a great future. I felt good about what I had achieved.

Rules and Regulations.

I think it reasonable to complain that anytime the government is involved in a program the rules and regulations multiply beyond sanity. Just look at the tax system in America as an example. When I was running LifePath I was inundated with regulations of all kinds, both fiscal and programmatic. There were State employees in Harrisburg whose job it was to write regulations, so of course that is what they did. It was what they were paid for. There was an Office of Quality Assurance whose staff honestly thought that they could achieve quality through the regulations they wrote. No amount of argument (or laughter) could persuade them otherwise. They were very serious people.

It is always difficult to decide which regulations make sense, and which are simply insane. When I was growing up in England my father typically had the same car for ten years or more. They never seemed to break down. I am sure my father had them maintained, but the important factor in their longevity was surely their simplicity. If you raised the hood you could see the engine sitting there, and any owner could change the oil and the spark plugs. There were almost no gadgets to go wrong, no heating or cooling system, no anti lock brakes, no on-board computers. When I came to America the first car I bought, which was an old Pontiac station wagon, was still pretty simple. All that has changed. Now if you raise the hood you cannot see the engine for all the stuff around it. I read a report on the recent Airbus crash which explained that the plane is flown by the computers, and if anything goes wrong it is very difficult for the pilots to correct the problem. I find this frightening. Presumably in the future they will do away with pilots altogether.

It is obvious that every time you add something, you add something which can go wrong. It is nice to have power steering, and power windows, and automatic transmissions, and climate control, and on board computers, but are any of them necessary? That is the question that should be asked. The other question that needs to be asked of course is how much will it cost. Everything added adds to the cost, and education is no different.

In January 2002 Bush signed the No Child Left Behind Law. The Law had several goals. One was to eliminate educational achievement differences between ethnic, racial, and economic groups. A second, allied to this, was to have all students achieve proficiency in reading and math by 2013. A third was to staff all schools with highly qualified teachers in at least the core subjects. As I write, the Law is up for renewal and there is much discussion. Needless to say, the outgoing administration is claiming success, but the success seems limited. There have been some improvements in scores, but the racial gap has not changed. The chances of all students reaching proficiency by 2013 seems to be a fantasy, as does the notion that whites and blacks and Hispanics will all be at the same level. There have been improvements in the number of highly qualified teachers, but that too is variable, and there remains enormous difficulty finding quality teachers for inner city and other difficult schools, and for the more difficult subjects like math and science. The best that one can say at this time is that the effect of the Law has not been dramatic.

Meanwhile in England the Labor government came to power in 1997 promising that it would revolutionize education. It certainly tried, but the results have not received universal praise. Cambridge University is currently issuing a whole series of research reports on primary education, and one of their conclusions is that Labor's tight centralized control has had a devastating and negative effect on children's education. Micromanagement, meddling, and a succession of ministerial edicts have killed all the spontaneity in the classroom. Teachers have been stripped of their powers of discretion, and the net result has almost certainly been a decline in the quality of education that the young receive. One report by Dominic Wyse concluded that government control of the curriculum and its assessment strongly increased from 1988 through 1997. "The evidence on the impact of the various initiatives on standards of pupil attainment is at best equivocal and at worst negative. While test scores have risen since the mid-1990s, that has been achieved at the expense of children's entitlement to a broad and balanced curriculum and by the diversion of considerable teaching time to test preparation." He goes on to argue that the quality of interaction between pupils and teachers has been particularly negatively influenced by the Labor government's approach which tells teachers exactly how to teach literacy and numeracy in primary schools. Teachers consequently no longer think on their feet, adapting lessons to particular needs, but instead follow a pattern which is choreographed from London.

It would seem, therefore, that in both America and England the central government has moved towards taking more and more control over education, with results that are far from overwhelming. Obama has already moved to take even more control, adding some five billion dollars to the education budget, and talking about closing 5,000 failing schools, as well as implementing a merit pay system for teachers. He is also on record as saying that everyone should have some form of post-secondary education.

The crucial issue is surely one of balance. The government can claim that they have to take over because the local educational structures are simply not delivering a quality education. On the other hand, government has a lousy track record of running anything.

The School Year

Many commentators have remarked on the absurdity of the school year, which basically consists of 180 days, with a long summer break, as well as breaks at Christmas and Easter. As everyone knows, this started because kids had to go back on the farm in the summer to help with the harvest. Farms have long since disappeared, but the school year has remained, another reminder of the deeply entrenched conservatism of the educational model in both countries.

I remember reading about a survey which found that the major reason why people went into teaching was the long summer vacation, and that is perfectly understandable, but we need to remember that the consumers are the students, not the teachers, and the question is what do they go into education for? There are a number of things than can be said about the 180 day year:

1.   What is it based on? What is the rationale? Frankly I do not think there is one. I do not think anyone ever sat down and said, this is what all children need to learn, this is how long it is going to take them to learn it, and therefore 180 times 7 hours it is. I think what happened was that the process started with the assumption of 180 days, and then said the learning process had to fit into that time scheme. In other words, it was plucked out of the air.

2.   Research has shown that different students learn at different rates. If we assume that all students (leave no child behind) will leave high school with the equivalent knowledge base, then it follows that different students will take different amounts of time to reach that level. Schools know that, but still compress all students into 180 days for 12 years because that is the way it has always been done. Because no one wants to keep kids back year after year, students tend to be passed up to the next grade whether or not they have mastered the material for the current grade. It is true that some schools require Saturday classes, and some schools require summer classes, but these are relatively rare. In Texas there was neither. The difference in academic achievement between the top students and the bottom students was enormous, but everyone graduated, with the exception of those students who simply left town.

3.   Research has also shown that the less intelligent students forget stuff over the long summer vacation. In September teachers therefore have to go over last year's material before they can start on this year's material. That is a waste of time

and effort, and also very boring for the students who have remembered the material.

4. Surveys have repeatedly shown that many students are bored stiff with school. This may be because the teachers are boring, or it may be that the students will be bored no matter what, but part of it must be the requirement that, for some students at least, the same material has to be gone over many times. In Texas my children learned multiple times all about cumulus clouds.

5. The fact that students learn at different rates is handled at the moment by permitting students to pass to the next grade if they get a C or better. In most schools a C is not much to shout about, and simply means that there is a wide gap between the students at the top of the class and the bottom, a gap which typically persists year after year. A student who graduates with a C average from an American high school has a very different knowledge set than a student who graduates with an A, but they have both graduated. In England students do not graduate from high school. Instead they sit a number of exams at various levels of difficulty, so that one student my have passed five, another three, and so on. Moreover the exams are in various subjects, so that there is some measure of what the student has actually studied and actually knows. American businesses and colleges are always complaining about students who have graduated high school but do not know how to read or write.

The solution would seem to be to allow the slower student more time to master the material. As there is a natural reluctance, for social reasons. to hold students back and make them repeat a grade, the alternative would be to give the slower students more days of education, ie to keep them in school beyond the magical 180. This would mean of course that teachers for these students would also have to teach beyond the magical 180. Doubtless this would meet with enormous resistance from teachers and their unions, but how else could it be done? Teachers who work 240 days would of course have to be paid more than those who work 180, but even the union would agree with that. The underlying assumption is that every student has achieved more or less the same level of learning on graduation, and that is never going to happen if all students are lock-stepped into successive 180s.

The Curriculum

Government is forever fussing around with the curriculum. In England, where there is much more central control than in America, this is particularly evident. Recently Ed Balls announced a new curriculum for primary schools. Managing emotions will have the same importance as English and math. Children will learn to take turns, to share, to prepare healthy meals, to manage their feelings, to work in teams, and to avoid drug and alcohol abuse. Expanded use will be made of 'circle time' where children sit facing each other for discussions of managing feelings, and 'worry boxes' where they will write down something that is worrying them and put it in a box for later discussion. Lessons will also center around six 'areas of learning' rather than the traditional disciplines, and there will be greater emphasis on speaking and listening skills.

The emphasis apparently is no longer on the transmission of knowledge, but instead on students developing a sense of responsibility for themselves, their health, their environment, their society; a respect and understanding for those from different backgrounds; and skills for learning and life. According to Mr. Balls, health and happiness matter as much as math and English.

The basic problem with this approach is that with 25% of primary school students failing to reach an appropriate level in math and English, the need is to rectify that problem, not replace it with a lot of psychobabble, which will inevitably take teachers away from the basic academic subject matter.

Feelings, emotions, anger, perceptions of right and wrong, attitudes to others are surely the prerogative of parents. It is true that some parents do a poor or incorrect job, but it is still their responsibility. The kinds of things mentioned above have always been handled by teachers as a matter of routine, not separated into their own little teaching modules.

In America there are similar intrusions into the academic

curriculum. There is Project DARE, which is meant to educate children against drug abuse. There is no evidence that this program is effective, but because it is a federal program it is implemented all over the country. Then there is Project Abstinence, which preaches abstinence as the only appropriate form of protection against HIV, other Sexually Transmitted Diseases, and pregnancy. The school in Texas put on this program every year. It was presented by an earnest young man who sounded as if he practiced what he preached, but once again there is no evidence that the program has any effect. Then of course there is the ongoing effort by various organizations seeking to add a course on creationism to the curriculum by arguing that it is a serious alternative to Darwin.

If there were evidence that the addition of these 'feel good' courses to the curriculum result in higher standards on academic subjects, then there would be at least an argument in support, but what evidence there is suggests that in fact the opposite is happening. Recent research in America suggests that the most important factor in turning low-performing schools into high-performing one is to raise the expectations of the children. Greg Wallace, head of Woodberry Down Community Primary School in Hackney, one of the poorest areas of London, says categorically that lectures on emotional development can do more harm than good. In six years his school has gone from weak to outstanding, and the critical factor has been raising expectations.

It seems only common sense to suggest that by the end of primary/elementary school all pupils should have all the knowledge and skills necessary to do high school work, and that by the end of high school all students should have all the knowledge and skills necessary to do college work, if that is the direction they are going, or all the skills necessary to pursue a vocational career. This currently does not happen.

In terms of preparation for college in America this can clearly be seen by looking at the Act results for 2009. About 1.48 million of the 3.3 million high school students took the test, and ACT looked at the results compared to the level predictive of college success in the various core subjects. 67% met the standard for English, 53% the standard for Reading, 42% the standard for Math, and 28% the standard for Science. In America students are required to take courses in all four areas when entering, and the results indicate that overall only 23% or a quarter of the students are college-ready. Given that students who take the Act are students who are at least thinking of college, although there are some States which require all students to take the exam, this is a woeful statistic, and means that all colleges offer remedial courses during the first year, courses which should have been mastered in High School.

Centralized versus Dispersed Control

Even though England has a population of 50 million, it is a very small country by American standards, able to fit nicely into one corner of Texas. Both countries clearly have a high degree of central control, with State Departments of Education. There are also differences. States in America are far more autonomous than Counties in England, and are very jealous of their States' Rights, and are wary of attempts by the Federal Government to control them. As a result States tend to resist attempts by the Federal Government to establish national anything, and the Federal Government has to attempt to bribe them into compliance, as Obama is currently doing. Additionally significant education funding comes from the States and school districts. Leaving that aside, governments always want to control, that is their nature. The question is, what is best for education, central control or local control?

If I were a superintendent, what would I want if I were asked to take over a school. I think I would want the following:

1. I would want a budget that is based on the number and type of students that I am charged with educating, and not on some curious local formula or historical accident. It is clear that different students have different needs and to have a one-size-fits-all approach does not work. How much should I be paid per student? I think that should be decided by the State, and should be common to all schools. Furthermore I think that the money should come out of State taxes and not out of local property taxes. Education is a common good. The amount per student should be evaluated each year based on some measure like the C.P.I.

I think that the States, not the Federal government, should take ownership of public education in the State, and that the competition should be between States, not within States. There needs to be pride at the school level, but there also needs to be pride at the State level. It is very difficult to have pride at the National level.

2. I would want to be able to hire and fire my staff at all levels. Education is a people business, and from the point of view of the student, the teachers are the most important people. You can have all the technology you want, the most beautiful and functional buildings, Olympic swimming pools, climbing walls, and so on, but unless the teachers can teach the students they have in front of them, it is all for naught. I would also want to be able to set staff salaries, staffing arrangements, and staff raises.

3. I would want to have clear objectives. I would want to know whether I was successful or not and I could only know that if the objectives were clear and measurable. I would want national tests so that I could evaluate how I was doing compared with other similar schools across the nation.

4. I would want to have a clear set of regulations. I accept the fact that there have to be regulations in various areas, but they need to be as limited as possible, and once again they need to be clear and measurable.

5. I would want to be able to purchase training as I saw fit and from whom I saw fit, and not have it imposed on me by some third party. I am not in favor of the State setting up regional offices which offer training which school staff then have to take, as mandated training quickly becomes banal.

6. I would want to have one boss. Many States are so large that they would probably have to have staff between the State Director and the various Superintendents, but their number should be limited.

7. I would not want a union.

8. I would want to take all students from whatever area I was responsible for. By this I mean that I should not be able to select. Private schools select who comes to them, partly through charging fees, but also partly by admissions standards of various kinds. There are various public schools in both countries which are also selective, because they were set up to be specialized. If all children have to be educated to a high standard, all children should attend quality schools. I would not abolish schools. My aim would be to make my school so good that parents would want their children to attend my school as opposed to an expensive private school.

9. I would want the school to educate all children from kindergarten through 12th. Grade.

10. I would want the school to offer both academic and vocational programs so that children could have a choice. I do not think everyone should go to university any more than I think every one should become an auto mechanic.

11. I would want to have the freedom to develop my own curriculum, and to staff it as I saw fit, given the needs of the students.

12. I would want to be able to operate all year round, as needed.

A student has a relationship with the school which he attends. A superintendent, principal, or headmaster has a relationship with the school that he manages. Neither has a relationship with the head of the national department of education in Washington or London, although of course the actions of the national department can have significant effects on both. The superintendent needs to take ownership of the school, and the student needs to feel that he belongs to the school and the school belongs to him. There has to be a process of identification, and ideally there has to be a long term relationship. If both superintendent and student are to be empowered, then they have to be empowered locally.

This raises the question of the role and power of the national department of education. Not so long ago there was no state department of education in either country, but once established they have steadily enlarged their power and scope, as governmental offices are wont to do. At this point in time in both countries they clearly see their role as dictating what education should look like, in fairly fine detail. While my natural inclination is to resist government interference, I do think that there is a role for a central entity. It should do the following things:

1. It should make sure that there are national standards. This is not a problem in England where national standards and exams have existed for some time, but in America there has always been tension between the Federal Government and the States. The result in the latter case is that standards of all kinds vary by State, so that what high school graduation means in Massachusetts is very different from what it means in Louisiana. The Leave No Child Behind law attempted to institute national tests by mandating that the National Assessment of Educational Progress be given at regular intervals across the country, in every State. But in a nod to States' rights the Federal Government allowed the States to use their own tests to measure whether students are improving. The result is widely differing results. In Mississippi for instance 89% of fourth graders performed at or above the proficiency level on the State reading test, but only 18 percent demonstrated proficiency on the federal test. Needless to say the State bureaucracy came up with a million reasons why this is an unjust comparison, supported to some extent by the Federal bureaucracy. It is true that there is an argument that the NAEP exam is set at too high a level, but the important objective is to have a examination which all students take and which allows for the comparison of students and schools across the nation. The relative powerlessness of the Federal Department can

be clearly seen in the case of the District of Columbia. This is the seat of the Federal Government, the home of the White House, and so forth, but the local school district is widely admitted to be one of the worst in the country. One result, for instance, is that even Obama immediately put his children into a private school! If the Federal Government cannot even deal with a school district in its back yard, how can it be expected to have much control of a school district in Texas? The nearest things to national exams in America are the ACT and SAT tests, which are taken when applying for college, and which are the same no matter where they are taken. Effectively they provide a common standard, at least for those students who are planning to go to college. The SAT also provides subject specific tests, thus being similar to the English A level exams.

2. It should define a core curriculum. This goes along with national standards of course. By a core curriculum I mean reading, writing, elementary math, and history. The ACT and the SAT essentially assume that there is a core curriculum, and the arguments about the curriculum seem to be mostly about what subjects should be taught in addition to the core. In an ideal world students should have classes in music and drama and art, and this would be easier in a longer school year and/or a longer school day. When my oldest child was a student in the Council Rock system in Pennsylvania (which was said to be an excellent school) she would have liked to have taken drama, but she was told that she was in the college track, and there was no time in her schedule for such an activity. There have been numerous arguments about curriculum as everyone seems to have an opinion, but it seems to me that when someone graduates from high school they should be a fluent reader, a fluent writer, reasonably fluent with numbers, and knowledgeable about the history of their country. When I taught at the college level I was always amazed at the number of students who had no idea how to write a term paper for the simple reason that they had never had to write one. Many of them

had no feel for language for the simple reason they did not read, or at least did not read good writing. It is one thing to understand the mechanics of grammar but it is quite another to have a feel for language – that you only get from reading authors who have that feeling. In Texas there was a constant refrain of 'I hate reading'. At Chelmsford Hall I won a number of prizes for academic work, and the prizes were typically nice editions of books – in my library I still have a couple of them, Sir Walter Scott's Ivanhoe, and John Buchan's Thirty Nine Steps. It seems to me that an ability to read and write must come at the top of any educational endeavor.

3. I think that is all the Federal Government should do. I think the best national government is the government that does the least, but does that well. The National Government should set the framework and then let people do their jobs. Clearly there are some areas where the national government, American or English, has to take total responsibility. The military is one, and international relations is another, and medical care is possibly yet another. Education in America I think should be left to the States, as should most other things, and within States to something like a school district, under one head. Politicians need to be accountable to the people who elect them, and the further they are away from those people the less accountable they become. Furthermore States, unlike the Federal government, have to work within their budgets. In addition all levels of government of whatever kind cost money, and education is an area where as much money as possible needs to go to the front line, which is the actual school. It will be argued of course that State governments are even worse than the Federal government, and in many cases this is doubtless true, but State governments are never going to improve unless they are given responsibility and power. If they become a welfare client of the Federal government, as in many cases they are, they will take on all the negative attributes of welfare

dependency, and every time something happens they will cry for help. Schools and children will suffer.

Tests

It is impossible to leave this area without a discussion of tests, probably the most contentious issue in education in both America and England. Teachers complain that there are too many tests, that they have to 'teach to the test' because they and their schools are evaluated on the basis of how many of their students pass the tests, that tests are destroying the beauty and creativity of education, that children are bored silly. In addition teachers resist being measured by how their students do on tests.

As a student I had no problem taking tests as I did well in them and welcomed a chance to show what I had learned. As a teacher I disliked giving tests, partly because I had to devise them, partly because I had to grade them, and partly because I had to tell at least some students that they had not done well. Nevertheless I do not see how one can do without tests of some kind. Both students and teachers need to know how they are doing and how they have done. Some kind of test is the only way to do this. I think therefore that the question is not so much whether there should be tests, but more how many, in what subjects, and how often.

All teachers at all grade levels give tests of various kinds as a matter of course. On the one hand this allows the teacher to find out whether the students are learning anything, and on the other hand it allows the students to know where they are. But in addition to these tests there are also external exams of various kinds, and it is these exams which the teachers complain about – they can hardly complain about their own tests! The number and frequency of these tests have increased steadily over the past 50 years as computers have made it easier to score them. A by-product has been the league tables, comparing schools against each other, which are now common in both America and England. The problem is compounded in America as I have said by the fact that States do their own testing, and these tests therefore vary between States – what counts as wonderful in one State may be lousy in another.

When I went to school I took external exams at age 11, 15, and

17. The exam at age 11 obtained my admission to Tonbridge, but also in general determined whether a student was seen as academic or vocational. The exams at age 15 secured my admission to Cambridge, always assuming that I had satisfactory marks on the exams I took at 17. At age 15 the exams I took were in English Language, English Literature, History, Latin, French (written and oral),German (written and oral), Elementary Mathematics, and Advanced Mathematics. At age 17 I took exams at an Advanced Level in French (written and oral), German (written and oral), and a General Paper. These were not the only courses I took, but the only courses in which I was externally examined. During my time at Tonbridge I also took courses in Science, Russian, Religion, and Art, but I did not sit examinations in those subjects.

A striking difference between the English and American systems of education is that in England there are no transcripts, no grade averages, no valedictorians, and no graduation ceremony. A student simply passes a desired number of exams, the number and quality of the scores signaling which university he will be able to attend. In addition, as in America, weight is given to recommendations, sporting achievements, leadership qualities, and so forth. In both countries, the better you do on these exams the better your chance of obtaining admission to one of the more illustrious universities, and the more scholarships you may be offered.

As I have said it seems reasonable to me that at the end of primary school – roughly at age12 – a student should be able to read fluently, speak fluently, write fluently, be knowledgeable about his country's history and culture, and competent in elementary math. Therefore at the end of primary school a student should be tested externally in those subjects. As the tests are external it is necessary that their coverage be known both by the examiners and the teachers and their students. No one can know everything, and American students should study American history and English students English history, and even then it is impossible to study all of history, so choices need to be made. As far as I can remember I studied Tudor history. I cannot remember reading anything about American history, nor do I see why I should have. Equally I read English classical literature, not American. The objective after all is to attain fluency in one's language and a love of reading. In Math the aim is to attain fluency and lose that fear of numbers which seems to such a curious and striking feature of modern students.

I would argue therefore for a traditional core curriculum, and national tests based on that curriculum, given at ages 12, 16, and 18. It is the responsibility of the teachers in the various schools to ensure that students are well prepared, and how they do that should be left to the teachers – that is where creativity comes in. All other subjects I would leave to be decided by the school. Every professional association wants their subject taught of course, so there is lobbying for geography, foreign languages, art, music, and so on. I took all these at Chelmsford Hall, but once in Tonbridge I started to specialize and concentrate on one area, which in my case was foreign languages.

I would also argue that it is better to do a few subjects in depth, than a multitude on the surface. There are all kinds of subjects which have interested me during my life, and which I never touched on at school. One day, when I was about 20, I happened to wander into a music store in Germany and on an impulse played a recording of La Boheme with Tagliavini and Carteri. I was entranced by it, and have been a lover of opera ever since – even though I can no longer play it, the recording remains on the shelf in my library! From there I passed naturally on to ballet, and classical music in general. I have spent considerable time over the years trying to decide whether there is a God or not, and if so, whether he is Christian! But perhaps the most curious thing is that I have never directly used any of my degrees.

Dumbing Down

There is some evidence that over time tests have become watered down in order that more students can pass them, rather than students being better educated so that they can pass harder tests which are meaningful. In 2008 the Royal Society of Chemistry in England devised a test which included questions from past tests, going as far back as 1960, and administered the test to 1300 of the country's brightest 16 year olds. The results showed that the older the questions, the less well the students did. Overall the average score was 25 per cent, but some students scored zero. Dr. Pike, chief executive of the RSC, attributed the results to the fact that students were not being taught how to understand the subject, but were simply being taught how to pass the test. Dr. Pike pointed out that students could get a good pass on present exams without having to do a single calculation, and consequently had simply acquired a superficial knowledge of the subject. Howard Gardner would doubtless concur with Dr. Pike. Gardner has argued in many books that students are not being taught to think, so that as soon as they are faced with material which is novel or which is presented in a way other than customary, the students flounder and cannot respond appropriately.

On the one hand it seems desirable that more and more students should be going to college, but on the other hand it would be nice to think that all college degrees meant the same thing. They do not. As more students attend college, more colleges lower their entrance standards, and sometimes do away with them altogether. Community Colleges typically only require that you sign on and pay up. They, like many other colleges, give new students tests which determine whether the students need remedial work in writing or math. If they do, then they have to take these courses before they proceed. The result is that the number of students attending college has gone up, but whether they graduate is another matter. At the University of Texas in San Antonio, for instance, only about 29% of the students have graduated with a degree after six years. It is impossible to say what has happened to the 71% who never get there. Some of course may have transferred to another college, some may still be plugging away, but probably most have simply given up, either because they need to work, or the material is too hard, or they get married, or whatever.

Academic versus Vocational

When I went to school there was a fairly clear distinction between those students following an academic track and those students following a vocational track. The divide was usually made at the end of primary school as a result of the 11+ exams. While there were discussions about whether the decision should be made later, and whether students should be able to change their minds (and their scores) at a later date, the basic idea that there were two kinds of students was a consensus idea. In those days, especially in England, there were few universities, and much less of a demand for degrees of any kind. My father had a successful career in Barclays Bank, and never went to college, and a friend of mine made himself into a millionaire, also in banking, also without a degree. On the other hand if you wanted to be a lawyer you had to get a degree, just like now. Over the years, as more and more students went on to tertiary education, more and more jobs required degrees whether they truly required that amount of education or not. In England and especially in American higher education became a boom business as both countries saw college education as a necessary path to personal and national economic success and growth.

I think it has been a mistake to disparage vocational education as compared to academic education. I do not believe that everyone either needs or wants to go to college, nor do I believe that everyone can benefit from three or four more years of college. Students should be able to choose which direction they take in life. Let me offer my wife's niece and nephew as examples. Their father is a truck driver, and dropped out of high school in order to follow that career. Of course someone with a degree does not regard driving a truck as a career, which is interesting in and of itself. Their mother started a florist's business in a farmer's market, and built it into a thriving business. Neither parent went to college. They live in a pleasant part of the world, a mix of country and urban settings. Both children went to the local public schools. The daughter loved every minute of school. She did well academically, but she also did well socially and in sports. She was the kind of student all teachers love to have, a pleasure to be around. Her mother tells me that she hated when school ended in June and could not wait for it to start up again in September. Because she loved school she obviously went to the next school, college. She went to Gettysburg College, a well respected institution, and earned a degree in sociology. As an undergraduate she worked as a dormitory supervisor. Because she aspired to a career in Higher Education, from Gettysburg she went to Virginia Polytechnic Institute and State University and earned a Master's Degree in Education, specializing in Higher Education and Student Affairs. On graduation she was hired by Bucknell University, another respected institution, as a Residential Life Coordinator, responsible for the management of five dormitories housing 660 students. Two years later she was promoted to Assistant Director in the Office of Housing and Residential Life, her current position.

Her brother hated school and would have dropped out had his mother not insisted he stay and graduate. He took as few academic courses as he could, as many vocational courses as he could, and 'apprenticed' himself while still in school. Once graduated he obtained his certification as an electrician and formed his own company. He currently has six employees and last year his company grossed 1.7 million! He is 24. Which sibling has done better? The answer is neither and both. They have both arrived at where they want to be at an early age. How did they get there? By knowing where they wanted to get.

Both Chelmsford Hall and Tonbridge were academic schools, so there was no vocational education of any kind. There were students who did not go to college, who went into business as salesmen or into their father's company, but the clear intent of both institutions was academic. This is not the case with the typical public school which obviously has a broad range of students of all kinds and of varying abilities. For that reason I would argue that public schools should have a strong vocational program, and that becoming a plumber should be as worthy a goal as becoming a teacher – and often better paid. The school in Texas had a minimal vocational program, even though most of its students were not planning on going to college. The result was that for many girls marriage still seemed to be the preferred goal, and pairing off at an early age was common. At the same time trying to find an electrician or a plumber to do work on one's house was almost impossible, and like many an 'educated' person I am totally incompetent when it comes to such work.

All academics tend to look down on work that is done with one's hands. When I was educated I clearly got the message that business was not valued, and Cambridge University had no business school at the time. Things have changed since then. Public schools however seem to blow hot or cold, but surely a vocational education is just as valuable as an academic one, and for many students, to be preferred. Finland, which does well on international tests, separates students into academic and vocational tracks in high school based on student grades.

It seems to make sense. While data still shows that overall people with degrees earn more over their lifetimes than people without degrees, a recent study in England found that 38% of graduates were not working in their field of choice.

Chapter Six

Education Beyond High School

" Education is what survives when what has been learned has been forgotten." B.F.Skinner,

In both England and America higher or tertiary education has been a growth activity since the end of the Hitler War. When I was growing up in England there were very few universities, they were of very high quality, and were difficult to get into. In America at the present time there are quantities of colleges and universities, some private, some public, of varying quality, some difficult to get into, some having virtually no admissions criteria at all. The government in England has announced that it wants 50 percent of students to go on to university, while in America that target has long ago been reached. What percentage graduate is another story, especially in America. Many colleges only graduate about 25% of their students.

Junior or Community Colleges

Uvalde is a town of about 16,000 in Texas about 45 miles from where I lived. On the edge of town there is a nondescript collection of buildings. They constitute the Southwest Texas Junior College. Junior or Community Colleges are two year institutions which greatly increased in number after the war. They typically serve their local area, and are mostly commuter schools with limited residential housing. About 36% of American college students attend junior colleges. They have a number of functions:

They provide Associate Degrees in various subjects, some of which are terminal. For instance you can get a degree in cosmetology, which will certify you to be a hairdresser. You can study auto mechanics, or nursing, or carpentry, or a number of other trades.

They also offer two years of college which are much cheaper than the standard four year model, and can be a stepping stone to a 'real' four year college. Many of the students in Texas, when they aspired to go to college, went first to a junior college, partly because it was cheaper, partly because admissions were not restrictive. In Alabama the local doctor's son is planning to go first to a junior college for two years, then to a university for a further two years, then to medical school.

They are remedial institutions, making up for the fact that so many students graduate from high school with limited skills.

As I have already explained, they provide on-line courses to local high schools so that their students can obtain college credit.

They serve older students who for one reason or another did not go on to college from high school, but have decided to 'go back'. Many students are part-time, largely because they need to work.

Community/Junior colleges come in all shapes and sizes. Some have splendid facilities, some not; some are small, some are large; some are specialized and serve only girls or young people looking for a career in the military; some are limited in their offerings, some expansive. None of them offer the wide array of programs offered by four year colleges, but on the other hand they are much less expensive. They offer certificate programs like cosmetology, but they also offer two year degrees in a variety of subjects, and offer a stepping stone to the next level. The question of course is whether they would be needed were high schools to perform at a higher level and also offer vocational programs, and if four year colleges were to be priced reasonably.

Obama in addition to trying to revamp the public schools, also wants to enhance junior colleges, boosting their graduation rates (which are dismal), improving their facilities (the Uvalde college is very unimpressive), and upgrading their technology.

England has something similar to community colleges, called sixth form colleges, which act as a bridge between high school and college proper.

The Implications of Dual Credit Courses

As I have said, students in Texas could take college courses for credit during their last two years in high school. This is a relatively new phenomenon in America. There are also courses called Advanced Placement, which are taken for college credit. Both these take place primarily online, with a qualified teacher taking multiple students, and often multiple students from multiple schools. In Texas many students signed up for these courses, for the obvious reasons that they were available, that they were funded by the school and not out of their own pockets, that they counted towards a potential future degree, and that the courses were in fact within their capabilities – in order to take the courses students had to pass tests in writing and arithmetic. Many students accumulated a year's worth of credits before they graduated from high school, which meant that they significantly reduced the time and expense of college, assuming that the college they went to accepted the courses towards their degrees, which most of them did.

The students in Texas were not outstanding so that it is evident that many students can start taking college courses at age sixteen. They would still be in high school, but their courses would be college courses and at age eighteen they could not only graduate from high school but could earn an associates degree at the same time. This would be funded through the high school's funds at no cost to the student. The student would then only need two more years to earn a bachelor's degree in a college of their choice, which would cut both time and money.

Not all students would be able to do this of course, because many of them would not pass the required placement exams in English and math, and those students would still have to progress through the normal high school curriculum in the hope that an extra two years would fine tune their skills to the point where they could enter college if they wanted to.

It goes without saying that many of the programs currently offered by community colleges could be offered during the last two years of high school. Why not? The average sixteen year old is certainly capable of learning auto mechanics, cosmetology, and so on. If they were certified in high school, once again they would save a lot of time and a lot of money, and their high school experience would be more motivational and enjoyable. At the same time many high school students are obviously capable of doing college work

Colleges and Universities

Colleges and universities have three functions. The first is to provide a place for serious scholars to do scholarly and creative work, whether in the sciences or in the arts. This function is not within the purview of this book, but I would like to point out that if this were the only function then we could get by with far fewer institutions. Most colleges, and most professors, in America and in England, never produce any scholarly work during their lifetimes.

The second function is to provide a place where students go to attain a higher level of learning, to obtain a degree. There is no doubt that having a degree increases one's earnings, so to the extent that this is true, colleges play an important role. Equally professors who are not scholars but who are great teachers have an important role here.

The third function, in the context of this book, is to host the professional schools of education which train teachers, and of course pursue research, and in some sense attempt to influence education at all levels,

Are Degrees Worth it?

When I went to Cambridge it was free, in the sense that the government paid for it, provided you got in. Recently the government installed fees, which are bound to increase as these things always do. In America, with certain exceptions, colleges have always charged fees, and they are increasing all the time. The result is that State colleges and universities now charge somewhere in the vicinity of $20,000, while private college charge $30,000 and up. As a result many students graduate with significant debt. This makes many poor students think twice about even going to college, even though the national government attempts to ease things with outright grants, and even though government continually preaches that more young people should go to college.

In 1975 Caroline Bird published a book entitled 'The Case Against College.' She made the following points:

- Many successful people did not go to college.
- If your father can afford to send you to Princeton, you would be better off if he bought you a business with the money.
- The cost.
- Many undergraduate degrees do not lead to a job – for instance history, sociology, philosophy, English.
- The argument that a college education is enhancing is nonsense.
- There is no evidence that going to college helps one with major life decisions.

Recently many of these arguments have echoed in England. A 2005 report in the Guardian reported that 38% of graduating students could not find work in their discipline. A 2007 report in the Telegraph found a similar situation. Unremarkably graduates with qualifications in law, medicine, education, and information technology found jobs in their field, but graduates with degrees in other areas often found themselves having to accept jobs which did not require a college degree of any kind. Universities make little effort to ensure that their degrees lead to jobs in specific fields – they know that undergraduate degrees in history, literature, sociology, psychology, and so on have little connection with the world of work.

My oldest daughter obtained a degree in communications, which is one of those degrees one takes if one is not sure what one wants to do. She ended up by working for the Association for the Blind, training nurses in how to identify vision problems in young children. She enjoyed the work, but it did not pay very much. Fortunately she made a good marriage, which solved that problem. My second daughter obtained a graduate degree in Business, and ended up with a job with Warner Brothers, which she liked. My son is currently taking a degree in history. He would like to teach history at the college level, which means he will need to get a doctorate in the field, so I hate to think how much debt he is going to incur. Of course, even if he gets his doctorate, there is no guarantee that he will obtain the kind of job that he wants – there are only a limited number of positions for historians.

I was fortunate in that when I went to Cambridge so few people went to university that a degree meant something special. When I graduated I felt I could do anything, which to some extent was true. It was this feeling that allowed me to walk away from jobs I did not like until I found one that I did like. I never directly used any of my degrees, but that was my decision. What my degree gave me was the confidence that I could do anything I set my mind to.

Do we need all these universities?

Another question which needs to be asked is whether we need all these universities? A 1997 study completed by the University of Kent in England found that a third of all graduates ended up in jobs which did not even need a degree, let alone a degree in their subject of study. There are plenty of anecdotes about Ph.D's driving taxis and so on. Both England and America seem intent on creating more colleges of all kinds which will simply make this problem worse.

Not all Degrees are the Same

Another problem is that not all degrees are equal. There is a huge difference between earning a degree at MIT for instance, and at the University of Texas in San Antonio, even though the piece of paper may look the same. Employers are quite aware of this difference, and hire accordingly. Recently a parliamentary inquiry in England showed that the number of students obtaining first class degrees had almost doubled in the last ten years, and argued that different universities required different amounts of effort to obtain similar degrees. It went on to argue that standards in universities needed to be radically overhauled so that there was a clear definition of what it meant to obtain a certain degree, so that similar degrees meant the same thing no matter the granting institution. Needless to say Diane Warwick, the chief executive of the universities' administrators organization argued that any attempt to establish nationwide standards would jeopardize the academic freedom so important to colleges. It seems however only sensible to know ahead of time what a particular degree is likely to be worth. Universities as degree granting institutions exist for their students, not for themselves.

At a recent conference Bill Gates urged colleges and universities to publish their graduation rates. He argued that institutions should be funded based on the number of degrees granted, and not on the number of students admitted. He also argued for universal achievement standards.

The fact is that everyone knows that a degree from Harvard or Cambridge is worth more than a degree from lower ranked institutions. The Conservative Party in England has said that they will publish exactly what a degree from which institution commands in terms of salaries. If that happens that will be interesting information. It is interesting to look at ACT scores in America. As I have said, the ACT is one of two exams, the other being the SAT, which aspiring college students take in order to apply to colleges of their choice. ACT publishes data which permits anyone who takes the exam to compare their results with national norms based, in 2008-2009, on a sample of 3,908,557. Scores range from 0 – 36. There are separate scores for English, Mathematics, Reading, and Science, and a Composite or Total score. Someone scoring 21 on the composite is better than 55% of people taking the test for example, or, if you like, worse than 45%. There is enormous variation between universities and colleges on what they will accept, which really comes down to what they have to accept if they are to fill their needed rosters. For instance at the present time I am looking for a college in Alabama for my daughter, who will be a senior in high school this year. The various colleges publish their admissions criteria, including the required ACT or SAT score. Needless to say, they vary all over the place. For instance to be eligible for admission to the Honors College at the University of Alabama you need a score of 28, which puts you in the top 8% of students nationally. At the University of West Alabama Honors College eligibility is 22, which means that you are better than 62%, or in the top 38% nationally. Either way you can claim to be an Honors Student, but obviously to be an Honors Student at the University of Alabama is much better than to be an Honors Student at the University of West Alabama. Why would anyone go to West Alabama if they could go to the University of Alabama? The answer is of course that they don't.

Jacksonville State University is even worse. They will accept students with scores of 16 on condition that they take remedial courses. A score of 16 means that you are only better than 19% of test-takers nationally. Jacksonville even has a summer program called Exsel for students with scores of 14-15 which gives them the opportunity to raise their scores if they can.

Obviously the better students go to the better universities and get hired for the better jobs. Equally obviously the better students are those who have attended better schools

The Liberal Arts Argument

There is an argument which says that going to university and obtaining a degree makes one a better person, especially if the degree is broad based, and not restricted in content. It is an argument which is elitist in origin and is based on the claim that for a person to be educated (at least in the West) he should be well versed in the origins of civilization, namely Greece and Rome, in classical literature, in music, and so forth. When my son received the Harvard Book Award the presenter dwelt at length on the value of a liberal arts education. In the presenter's opinion, a broad based education encouraged a person to think for himself, to think outside his domain, to develop values which were universal in scope, and to appreciate other cultures and thought systems. It is worth remembering that universities were originally set up by the rich for the rich, and their intent was to produce gentlemen, and part of the definition of a gentleman was that he (there were no she's) should be classically educated.

If neither cost nor time were an issue then I would agree with the liberal arts argument Spending four or three years taking a smorgasbord of courses in various areas while living on a pleasant campus with unlimited food, numerous specimens of the opposite sex, and a plenitude of extra-curricular activities, is difficult to beat. At the same time you have four months a year when you can go to the beach or to Italy or even possibly obtain a summer job

But cost is an issue, and time is an issue. Moreover I am not convinced that spending four years in a typical American college or university guarantees that one receives a liberal arts education. My son is currently attending the University of Alabama. As I have said, he wants to study history. So in his freshman year he took a course in Greek and Roman Mythology, a course in Advanced English Composition, a course in Western Civilization, a course in Italian, a course in Finite Math, a course in Ancient Egypt, and a course on Fascism. Next year he is taking more Italian, and courses in Western Civilization, American History, and English Literature. As an undergraduate degree in history is almost worthless, he will have to go on to graduate school. The son of a friend of mine who is a doctor went to St John's College in Maryland, which is as liberal arts as you can get as they spend four years studying the Great Books. When I asked the son what he was going to do with that degree, he told me he is going to law school.

I would argue that if taking liberal arts is so important, then it should be done in high school. Why not? In England one goes to university to study a subject, so that liberal arts education takes place in high school. That was where I was exposed to the subject such as it is, and while Tonbridge is an elite institution, you do not have to be an intellectual genius to study the history of western civilizations and other similar courses. In a typical high school you could still take your core courses in English and Math and Science, and make everything else an elective, thus freeing up time. Languages and social studies and similar programs should be electives. The fact is that schools should concentrate on teaching students how to read and write and think. If they can truly do that then they can learn what they want to learn, in school or out, and you would have people truly ready to be life long learners.

If liberal arts however defined were done in high school, then college could be reduced to three years at the maximum, which is the norm in England. When I took my law degree I only actually studied law for two years – the first year I studied German and French – and earned a B.A. and an M.A. Furthermore I took only courses in law after the first year. It is customary in England to go to college to study a subject, and thus become an expert in that subject. In the typical American college a student does not have to declare a major until their junior year, so the fact is that most of them also obtain their degrees based on two years studying a specific field.

Furthermore in America most colleges offer courses in what they call pre-med or pre-law, and so forth. They start with the assumption that you have to continue your schooling for at least two more years. If they dispensed with all the other courses they require you to take, then you could go straight from high school to medical or law school or any other professional school, and save a lot of money and a lot of time. You could still decide that studying medicine requires more time than studying other subjects, but I am personally not convinced that this is so.

As I have said, most American high schools are already offering college courses to their students. In Texas, as I have noted, students could take on-line courses at the local junior college (a two-year institution) starting in their junior year, and many students did this, thus getting a jump on their college careers as they earned genuine college credits which were applicable to the degree courses they would take later (subject of course to the approval of the four year college!!) Students could also take Advanced Placement courses, also on-line, and also eligible for college credit provided their score was high enough. In essence these avenues meant that a student could earn a year's worth of college credit before they ever left high school.

For this to have genuine effect high schools will have to change of course, offering courses other than the ones they now offer, but the presence of the internet now makes all this possible.

In my own case Tonbridge School gave me a liberal arts education. I not only studied languages as languages, but I studied the literature of the languages I studied. In fact reading the literature was the chief method of learning a language. So I read Racine, Corneille, Racine, Moliere, Beaumarchais, Goethe, Schiller, Lessing, and so on. The books I used are still in my library. My experience with American high schools is that languages are taught, but as languages, on the assumption that the aim is to be able to speak them. You can of course do this much more easily by spending six months in the appropriate country. My son took three years of Spanish in Texas and learned nothing. It bored him. The way to learn to speak a language is to live in the relevant country.

All this means that the American high school needs to change. It needs to be more academic for those students who want to go that route, and it needs to be more creative and intellectual if I may use those words. Money should be taken away from colleges by the simple method of reducing the time spent there, and directed to enhancing high schools. Colleges could then become professionally oriented, and become what are now graduate schools in America.

As I see it, all children would go to primary school and learn to read, write, add, and think. At the end of primary school they would be tested to ensure that that had the desired competencies and skill sets, and would then go on to high school. High schools would have a far broader range of subjects than they currently do. Students would still have to take courses in English and math, but other courses would be electives, and could include not only science but such thing as drama, history, geography, or music. In high school English should be English or American literature so that students could develop an ear for appropriate language use, as well as learning about their country of origin. High schools should have three terms – fall, spring, and summer – adding up to something like 220 days, thus allowing slower students to receive additional tutoring if need be and brighter students to take additional courses for college credit. The aim would be for all students aspiring to go to college to attain an appropriate level. Meanwhile all high schools should offer a serious vocational program for students who choose to go in that direction. Students should be able to switch between the college and vocational tracks during their high school years if they change their minds or their abilities. Colleges could then focus on preparing students for their professional career of choice, and would graduate lawyers, doctors, accountants, scientists, writers, professors, and so forth, and would do that in three years unless it was very clear and substantiated through research that the particular skill needed additional time – although of course colleges also work on the 180 day year, which could also be changed.

I think that many skills professionals use in their work are best learned on the job and not in the classroom. In fact many people never directly use their college degrees – I used mine full-time for only three years when I taught at the University level. I would therefore also urge that all students in high school do a certain amount of applied work. Clearly this should be especially true for plumbers, electricians, and welders, but would also apply to would-be accountants, lawyers, and doctors. Once in college there should be even more of this so that students could actually see how the real world functioned and perhaps be either entranced or disillusioned. The fact is that many people only learn the job when they are working at it, and there is nothing wrong with that. I asked a doctor as he tested my lungs how he could pick up if something was wrong. He said that after he had listened to a thousand pairs he just could.

The tremendous advantage of making high school a hot-bed of education is that they are already funded and therefore free to the students, although their enhancement will take a few more dollars/pounds. Colleges would be made cheaper simply by reducing the time spent in them and possibly reducing their number.

Online Education

There is of course another way of reducing the cost of obtaining a degree and that is not to go to college at all in the traditional sense, but to do everything online. This is happening more and more as people are beginning to realize that it is much cheaper, you can work from home, you do not have to pay outrageous prices for dorm rooms and meals and climbing walls, and you can move at your own speed. Moreover you can do it at any time. A friend of mine in England took a degree online in her seventies – she grew up in an era when daughters did not go to college. Modern children spend half their waking hours glued to their computers so the technology is easy for them, and just think – they could actually spend some time learning something useful as opposed to playing endless games.

Obama has declared that everyone should have some form of post-secondary education. I think he is mistaken. I think everyone should learn to read and write fluently – and I underline the word fluently – by the end of primary school, that they should receive a liberal arts education in high school or alternatively a rigorous vocational education ending with an appropriate certificate, that they should be well prepared academically or vocationally by the end of 12th grade, and that they should then study a field of their choice intensively for no more than two years, and learn the rest of their trade or profession on the job, which is what most people do anyway, unless they plan to be a pure academic. The present college system is organized more for the benefit of the colleges than their students, and this not only needs to change, but will inevitably change because of economic pressures.

Chapter Seven

Research in Education

"...the situation in educational research is scandalous." Nisbett

"Nothing in education is so astonishing as the amount of ignorance it accumulates in the form of inert facts." Henry Brooks Adams

There is a mass of information in education, but hardly any of this information leads to knowledge about what works, about what will improve student achievement. The result is that there is a lot of floundering about, and stances which seem to change every decade or so. For instance there is still a lack of clarity on how to teach reading to young children, whether phonics is the way to go, or whole language, or something else. How can this be after all this time? It is because there is a general lack of consensus on almost all things educational, so decisions are made not on the basis of demonstrated effectiveness, but on the basis of opinion. In 2006 in England Jim Rose was charged with examining the way English children were taught to read. On the basis of his observations he recommended that synthetic phonics should be required. This method teaches the 44 sounds of the English language before introducing books. As soon as this was announced it came under attack from various quarters. The Early Years Curriculum Group claimed that teaching phonics to children under six was unrealistic and boring, and that the research used to support the method was limited and faulty. Meanwhile Dr. Bousted of the Association of Teachers and Lecturers said that while phonics had a role to play, it should not be the start of the process. This kind of argument is par for the course in education. Everything becomes a matter of opinion, rather than a matter of fact.

One problem of course is that it is very difficult to do experimental research in education. This research requires randomly assigning students to two groups, one of which would receive the experimental condition, and one of which would not. For instance one group would be taught using phonics and the other group would be taught using whole language. As outcomes in education do not occur rapidly but take a number of years to validate researchers become nervous. Furthermore the researcher has to obtain approval from multiple sources, including parents. What if their children are in the group which does less well? When I was preparing to research my doctoral dissertation I thought of using the Philadelphia School System as my base. My advisor told me in the strongest terms not to even try. I would have to pass through so many hurdles, he said, that it might well delay my doctorate by a couple of years!

Public education is very much a political football. It is a huge item in any budget, and every politician has to say how much he or she supports it, but it is funded through taxes of various kinds and competes with everything else that is funded through taxes. There are other huge items in any budget, including health care, military expenses, old age supports, and so on. In both England and America politicians promise to deliver vast improvements in their educational systems, and are surprised when it does not happen. But politicians rarely understand what they are talking about, and think that it is enough that they went to school so obviously they understand education! Furthermore the people in charge of education at the national level change every few years, so there is little consistency. In America President Bush signed the Leave No Child Behind legislation, which produced a lot of mandates which were imposed on local schools, but so far seems to have had little effect apart from rhetoric.

The fact is that we simply do not know how to educate children who do not wish, for one reason or another, to be educated, and it often seems that we are not interested in knowing, despite all the fine words. This is why if you are going to change a school, you need to hire an outstanding leader. If you knew how to teach low-achieving students, then you could simply apply that knowledge across the board, and be done. In Texas there was the obligatory statement to the effect that all educational interventions had to be research based, but the statement was meaningless because there is so little research which impacts local schools in any meaningful way. Most Superintendents, Principals, or Head Teachers simply do not know the research that there is, which tends to circulate only among academics, and teachers certainly do not read or implement research findings: they depend on others to tell them, and then grumble.

This is not because there is no research, but because most of the research that is carried out has nothing to say about real life problems in the classroom. In 2006 a group of academics established a new research group called the Society for Research on Educational Effectiveness which would focus on advancing scientifically rigorous research. Its Advisory Board included professors from various high ranking universities. Immediately after it was formed, other academics questioned the need for such a group, given that there already existed two large groups which were meant to focus on such issues, the American Educational Research Association, and the National Academy of Education, both based, needless to say, in Washington, D.C.

Given the absence of clear research findings everything becomes a matter of someone's opinion. For example in Education Week May 24th 2006 there was a discussion between Deborah Meier and Diane Ravitch. Both were professors at New York University at the time, and both have decades of experience in the field. While they have areas of agreement, they also differ on some major issues. Diane for instance argues for a national curriculum and national standards. She claims that the curriculum that most schools currently teach is already a national curriculum, but a curriculum which is characterized by mediocrity and superficiality, based on boring text books, and assessed by banal tests. Deborah agrees that the current curriculum is boring and superficial, but believes that the solution is to give local schools and families more power about not only the content of the curriculum, but how to teach it. In other words, Diane prefers a top-down approach while Deborah prefers a bottom-up one.

Obviously there are arguments for both approaches but the arguments are based not on anything that might be called research but rather on what one might call philosophical views of what education should be about and how it should be organized.

Apart from research on what actually works, even basic descriptive data is flawed. As an example, historically States all had their own way of establishing drop out rates, and most of them cheated so that their high school graduation rate looked good. When the Bush administration looked into this it found that published rates were far higher than actual rates. For instance when North Carolina adopted a more rigorous formula its graduation rate plummeted from 95% to 68%. It seems that graduation rates in most States hover around 70%, or, to put it another way, every year 1.2 million Americans drops out of high school. In some ways this information is even more disturbing than the fact that American students do worse than some other nations on various international tests

Chapter Eight

It is time to try to summarize my conclusions. But before I do that, let me tell you what the new Secretaries of Education in England and American are planning to do.

Ed Balls in England has stated that he will:

Introduce a new 'license to teach' similar to a new system for doctors and lawyers, under which teachers will be assessed regularly at least every five years. Presumably teachers who do not pass will either undergo some form of re-training or will lose their license.

Provide one-on-one tutoring for all students who are performing below the expected level at age 11, which is as I have noted about 25% of children. The effects of this tutoring will be assessed on a regular basis to ensure that it is having the desired effect.

Redirect money to schools in the poorest areas of the country. This could mean that schools in richer areas could lose funding.

Evaluate schools on six factors: pupil progress, pupil attainment and well-being, parental and student perceptions of the school, and how well the gap between the rich and the poor is being reduced.

Provide relevant and challenging learning to every student, and give extra support to students who demonstrate particular talents.

Oblige parents to support their children's school

Develop a process whereby good Headmasters are given control of more than one school.

Decrease central control and give more power to individual Headmasters to drive up standards.

Arne Duncan, his equivalent in America, has said he will:

Close thousands of the countries worst schools, and reopen them with new staff. Existing teachers would have to reapply. As Mr. Duncan does not have the authority to close schools – this remains a prerogative of local authorities – he will have to negotiate with local power structures, and, of course, the two unions.

Provide billions of dollars of new money, and use this money as a carrot to persuade local authorities to accept new initiatives.

Expand charter schools, which are essentially state-funded schools without all the baggage.

Foster school choice in one way or another.

Pay teachers based on their performance.

Increase funding for community and other colleges.

Increase post-secondary school education of all kinds.

Develop common academic standards.

Increase class time, by increasing the school week and the school year.

I might point out that both Balls and Duncan serve 'liberal' governments, but while Duncan may have power for another eight years, Balls will probably be out of a job within twelve months. It will be interesting as always in politics to see how much of their agenda they can achieve.

I have difficulty perceiving education as a serious endeavor. This might seem to be an extraordinary statement, but how else do you explain a system which in both America and England has been failing thousands of students for decades. In both countries successive governments have claimed that they are going to change things, and in both countries, after the expenditure of significant sums of money, all that has been changed is the frills, the main education world chugs along just as before. The reason is that to my mind many of the things which need to be done are common-sensical, but they nevertheless do not get done because of the basic inertia in the system. It is of course a huge system, and most of the current players benefit by the lack of change, so why should they agree with anything that might upset that? As soon as anyone suggests lengthening the school year, for instance, the education world screams in horror. It would cost too much, it would achieve too little, and so forth and so on. When I was at Saucon a local group wanted to develop a Charter school. The Saucon administration acted as if the end of the world was coming. The Charter school would siphon off the best students, the Charter school would take away funding, the Charter school would hire away the best teachers, and so on. No one suggested that choice and competition might be a positive thing, might be a challenge for Saucon to do a better job, might be better for some students. No one explained why, if Saucon was so good, how the Charter school could be a threat. It was just unacceptable. Saucon was a monopoly, and that was how it should be. The problem that this creates is of course that there is lots of talk, but little action. There is lots of fussing around with the details, but the basic structure stays the same, and if the basic structure stays the same it is difficult to see how it can significantly improve.

In a speech to the National Conference of State Legislatures Bill Gates said that the American educational system was wedded to old beliefs and bad habits. He said we cannot come up with the correct answers until we ask the right questions. He said that there had to be uniform achievement standards and uniform measurement of those standards. He said that colleges should publish their graduation rates, and that teachers should be rewarded for effectiveness. He said that education was the sector of the economy which was the least changed by technology, and that technology should be embraced at all levels.

Let us look at the challenges and some of the things that need to be done.

Students

In all countries children come to school with a culture, a set of values and attitudes which defines their initial relationship with the school, their teachers, and their peers. They have learned these values from their parents and the culture in which their parents live. If these initial values view education negatively the major and most important task of the school is to change that culture. This is almost impossible at the present time. Children spend at most 12% of their time in school. The rest of the time they are at home or with their peers, and even in school they are with their peers. For the school to somehow overcome this discrepancy is a challenge which is rarely met. Countries which rank high on the educational ladder tend to be countries which have common cultures which support education no matter the social standing of the family.

The issue of culture is exacerbated by the issue of poverty. Poor people see the world differently from rich people, and one part of the world that they see differently is education. For the children of rich parents education is a necessary process which they rarely question, and which is built into their culture. They understand that to succeed in the kind of life to which they aspire they need to do well in school. They are willing to do what it takes to do this, and of course they are supported by the simple fact that their parents are supportive both emotionally and in terms of hard cash. Poor children do not have these advantages, and often do not see going to college as an option. For rich children high school is simply a stepping stone to college; for poor children it is merely a stone.

When I came to America in 1965 I was, as I have said, enthralled by the notion that Johnson was going to do away with poverty. 40 years later poverty is still with us, in both countries. While the exact amount varies from year to year, and while there are arguments about how exactly it should be measured, there is no doubt that many students live in poverty, and come to school from environments which are impoverished. All homes have televisions, and ipods abound, but books are foreign objects.

Both England and America lack a common culture at the present time, and it is possible that this lack of a common culture is increasing. When I grew up in England there was a far greater degree of cultural cohesion than there is now, simply because of the lack of significant immigration. The population was all white. Football teams and cricket teams were all white and their members had all been born in England. Teams represented their towns and neighborhoods. Now teams are made up of players from all over the world. I still experience a shock when I read of an English Olympic Champion and click on her photo to find that she is colored. Somehow I still assume that to be English means to be white. That was the culture I grew up in. America of course is a country of immigrants, the original inhabitants having been reduced to the margin, but even in America 'high culture' is defined as the culture of the original States.

In America there is the additional problem of race. Blacks, as a group, have been mired at the bottom of society for the whole of their history, and there has been little change over the years. Latinos, whether they are from Mexico or Puerto Rico, have moved ahead of them, and are also becoming more numerous and therefore politically more powerful. In my forty years in America there have been many attempts to level the playing field, from forced bussing to race quotas, but nothing has made a significant long term difference. It would seem to be a problem which will be solved only when poor blacks take matters into their own hands, and accept responsibility for their own fate. Increasing numbers of blacks are moving into the middle class, but so far this seems to make little difference in the basic picture. There are now black mayors of major cities like Philadelphia, but black poverty continues, and black kids as a group continue to languish at the bottom of every educational measure of achievement. The center of American government is located in one of the worst cities in the country from an education point of view, a city whose residents are mostly black.

One solution which has been suggested is to place kids in residential institutions away from their culture, but my experience at Hutton Poplars suggests that they would simply bring their culture with them. There are programs which identify talented students in the public schools and set up special programs for them, and these are to be encouraged, but do not alter the basic picture. The solution would seem to lie in the hands of the parents and the schools. Schools and parents have to work together to educate their children. The problem is that poorer parents are less likely to be prepared to do this. After all, schools and their staff are very middle class, and live in a different world than poor parents.

Parents

Culture is handed down from parents to children. Schools therefore need to do what they can to connect with poor parents, and persuade them that their children can succeed in life, can go to college. Both

Chelmsford Hall and Tonbridge were largely boarding schools, although Tonbridge admitted a significant number of day students from the local area. Neither school had to make any effort to persuade parents of the value of education – parents had already put their money where their values were. At Swain there was a significant effort to involve parents because the school depended on fund raising for new buildings and other things. At Saucon the school had mandatory meetings between the homeroom teacher and parents twice a year. At both Swain and Saucon parent volunteer groups were heavily involved in sports programs, especially at the junior grades. But these were all schools that were preaching to the choir.

When we arrived in Texas I asked one of the teachers why there was no PTO. She replied that there had been, but the teachers ended up doing all the work, so it was discontinued. I set up personal meetings with all the teachers who had my children in their classes, and the teachers were perfectly willing to meet with me, but there was no attempt to do this as a regular feature of school life, even though many of the parents clearly did not value education, and needed to be talked to in the hope that they would become more involved and more positive. Once when I was meeting with the principal he joked that people had been asking what my problem was. They assumed that parents only requested meetings in order to complain!

Parental involvement in Texas was therefore minimal, and the school had essentially given up on any attempt to persuade parents that schooling was important. As I have said, when I arrived there I was told that only the teachers' children went to college, and it was alleged that this was racist, but in fact the reason was simply that the teachers (obviously) valued education, and instilled this value in their children. The fact that they were all white did not help of course. Most of the poor children, both white and Hispanic, simply drifted through school for 12 years (or disappeared at some point) and when they graduated went into menial jobs, which was what they expected out of life.

Influencing parents is a difficult task. All schools these days have counselors with various titles but they seem to do little in this area. Texas had a counselor but did almost nothing to encourage students to go to college – this was left to the parents. This meant of course that if the parents were not interested their children were not interested. Few students went on to college.

If the low educational aspiration and achievement of poor and/ or minority children is to change, schools not only have to do a far better job of preparing such children, but someone has to educate their parents and change their culture. This has never been done on a nationwide scale to my knowledge. It is obviously a huge task.

Unemployment or underemployment is also a huge problem. If someone earns a reasonable wage and has a steady job, then it is much easier for them to see a future for their children, and much easier for the children to see a future for themselves. If on the other hand parents do not have stable jobs and rely on welfare to survive then the picture that their children see must surely be a negative one. How can someone delay gratification when they have so little gratification to begin with.

Hence the need for jobs. Currently the United States and England are struggling with the fall out from the economic crisis but even before that full employment was an ideal rather than an actuality. If a nation is to flourish it must encourage job creation, and not simply among the bureaucrats but among the real business and commercial world. If there were jobs available there would still be people who would be unemployed but they would be a very small minority. The disappearance of unemployment would, I think, have a powerful effect on both parents and their children. It would also do away with poverty.

Teachers

From the point of view of the student the teacher is the most important component of the entire educational system. This can work both ways. A teacher can change a student's life for better, but he can also change it for worse. The task is to make sure that every teacher changes students for the better. That is also a large task and a number of things have to be done if it is ever to be accomplished.

First of all we need to do away with unions. Unions represent teachers, not students, and therefore always distort the primary goal of education, which is to teach kids. Unions defend and protect bad teachers, and that should never be allowed. Furthermore teachers have the right to strike, and strikes in human services should not be allowed. How can you claim to be an educator and care about kids if you are willing to desert your students at the behest of a bunch of union officials?

Secondly there is no evidence that teachers who have degrees from colleges of education are any better than teachers who do not. So the current college education departments should be scrapped. Teachers should major in the subject they are going to teach, and should then be assigned to work with a 'mentor' teacher in an actual school where there are real kids who need to be taught, and who do not necessarily agree with submitting willingly. Teaching is a craft apart from anything else, and the best way to learn how to handle a classroom is to work with someone who knows how to do it. Sitting in a classroom being lectured at by someone who has earned a doctorate in order to get out from teaching in a public school is a waste of time.

Thirdly teachers need to be freed up to do their job, which is to teach. We need to throw away a lot of the paper that is dumped on them in order to provide statistics to some administrator and beyond, and we need to allow teachers to teach, in which ever way suits their particular personality and view of life. There need to be national objective exams so that we know whether students are learning, but these exams need to be limited to the core subjects of English, math, and science. If students have mental health problems they should be referred to a community agency. If students have significant behavioral problems, then they should be placed in classrooms set up to deal with these behaviors. If they are so out of control that they attack teachers, then they should be dismissed from the school, taken to court, and placed in a specialized setting until they are ready to come back to school.

Fourthly teachers should be required to meet on a regular basis with the parents of their students and parents should be required to attend these meetings.

Fifthly teachers need to accept that their job is to teach, and that it is reasonable to assess whether they are succeeding or not.

Sixthly teachers should accept that they need to do whatever it takes to ensure that their students learn the material. If this means tutoring in the evenings, additional lessons in the summer, and extended school years, so be it. Only educators define full time work as eight months a year.

Schools

When you think about it, there is something absurd about the fact that schools have changed so little in one hundred years, and that the same model is used whether the students are like those at Tonbridge or those in Texas. What works in one place does not necessarily work in another – schools need to be formatted to their students, and not the other way around.

I must confess, as I have already said, that I perceive a certain lack of seriousness in public education. This might seem to be a surprising thing to say when so much money is spent and so many people are employed and so many words are spilt, but I believe that education overall needs to make a decision as to whether or not it is serious about educating every student.

Private schools like Chelmsford Hall and Swain and Tonbridge by definition are not serious about educating everyone, they are only serious about educating the students they accept. This makes their task much easier of course, but at least they are serious about that task. They feel it as a personal affront if they do not succeed in educating their students. Public schools on the other hand, in my perception, while they have a much more difficult task, in essence do not accept that their task is to educate all the students that come to them, but rather they see their task as educating those students who want to be educated, and even those up to a very low standard. Public schools reflect the students that they serve, and cases where a public school has changed its students from low-functioning to high-functioning are rare.

I would argue that students should not pass out of primary school unless they achieve an appropriate skill level in English and math and basic science. This currently is not done. All students are passed on to the secondary school on the argument that no one wants to see a six foot tall 16 year old in primary school. It is true that this would be something to avoid, but the way to avoid it is to ensure that that student, and every other student, achieves the desired level. Cambridge only works if Tonbridge does its job, and Tonbridge only works if Chelmsford Hall does its job, and so on. All these schools are independent of course so they can simply reject students who do not have the correct skill level. Is there any reason why primary/elementary schools cannot bring all their students to an appropriate level of literacy by age 11?

I therefore think that every effort should be make to ensure that primary schools do their job, and that primary schools should accept that responsibility, whatever it entails. Education is cumulative, and for that reason the earliest years are the most important. If additional money is to be put anywhere it should surely be put into the elementary primary schools. I recently attended a meeting at a local college where my daughter was planning to take some courses while still in high school. The staff person from the college started to talk about the need to take notes and about how to do that. I realized with some degree of shock that she assumed that after eleven years of schooling the students did not know how to take notes. What was even more shocking was the thought that she might be right.

Secondly the school year needs to be changed. It is absurd to believe that all students can learn the same things in 180 days (less time off for things like football matches). Recently a young girl came in to the store to look for a job. Her father had just died and she needed to work. She was sixteen and entering her senior year in the local high school. She said her time was flexible because she had completed all her coursework by the end of her junior year, and would have no formal classes. Presumably she was high in acintel, and had simply outstripped her classmates, but she nevertheless has to stay in school another year in order to graduate. It does not make much sense. If she had done all her work, why can she not graduate now, or is all important that she go through that American rite of passage with her classmates? In England the situation is more flexible in that there is no such thing as graduation, you simply leave school when you are ready, and that is defined by the moment when you have passed all the external exams that you need to, which in turn depends on what you are going to do next. If you are going to college, then your need is different than if you are going into the family firm. In many ways school are organized on magic principles, on the notion that there is something unique about 12 years at 180 days a year. I do not understand why. I cannot find a single piece of evidence which says that the school year should be

180 days. It is perhaps the biggest chunk of evidence that the system is in a state of inertia. There are countries of course where the school year is longer than 180 days and the school day is longer, and every time a country does well on international exams American and English educators fly off to see how they do it, and come back and carry on as before.

Thirdly schools need to be relieved of the same paper-work and extraneous activities that teachers need to be relieved of. The job of the principal is to support and encourage his teachers in the task that they are called upon to do. Educators talk all the time about creativity, but few of them are very creative. Teachers quickly relapse into routine processes where they teach the same material year after year, in the same way. Creativity is in how you teach, not what you teach. Similarly schools need to think creatively about what they are doing, and how they are doing it. Teachers are always complaining about the regulations and rules which are imposed on them from outside, but this all happens because no one trusts them to do their job without outside pressure.

Fourthly principals need to be supported in the job that they have to do. Just as teachers are responsible for their students' outcomes, so principals are responsible for their school's outcome, and there is no way around that Just as teachers need to demonstrate that they are succeeding in their task, principals need to demonstrate that they are succeeding in theirs'.

The Bureaucracy

Simply put, there should be as little bureaucracy as possible. Why can Chelmsford Hall and Tonbridge exist independently, while the school down the road has to be surrounded by bureaucracy? I accept the fact that anyone who provides you with money has a right to know how the money is being used, and that it is being used to the right end. I accept the fact that there needs to be some way to evaluate whether a school is doing its job. What I do not accept is these requirements interfering with the school's primary task. The government sends its inspectors in to Tonbridge just as they send them into the local state school. Tonbridge's academic results are compared to every other school's, private or state. That is as it should be, and that is where it should end. The inspectors should not tell Tonbridge teachers how to teach, or which text books to use, or which novels to read. That is the job of the Headmaster and his staff. In the same way the bureaucracy should not tell the Principal of the public school how to do his job.

It must be remembered that every dollar or pound spent on a bureaucrat is a dollar or pound taken away from educating kids. Bureaucrats do not see it that way of course, and never have. They convince themselves that they have an important role to play, but it is difficult to define what exactly that role is. In America in addition to the State Offices of Education there are regional offices littered all over the landscape, costing money in terms of buildings and staff, but what do they do that in fact moves education forward? No one knows.

Higher Education

Higher education is becoming too expensive and too time consuming. Something needs to give. While it is still true that having a degree is an advantage economically, this advantage will decline as more and more people obtain degrees, and has to be balanced against the increasing debt incurred by many students. Furthermore the increasing expense is a barrier to the hope that increasing numbers of minority and poor students will pursue higher education.

I would argue therefore that high schools should offer programs that are currently offered in junior colleges, and that the latter could be dispensed with in their current role, which is largely remedial in an attempt to address the deficiencies of the high school. High schools should become far more rigorous that they currently are, so that graduation is a significant achievement, and means, among other things, that the student can actually read and write fluently, which would do away with the remedial aspect of junior college.

If high school had serious and rigorous vocational programs then many of the trades that are currently learned at junior college, like cosmetology and auto mechanics and nursing, could be taught in the last two years in high school.

Colleges and universities are elite institutions, and are fine when they are dealing with elite students who can pay the fees and can afford to spend years obtaining a degree and enjoy climbing walls and Olympic swimming pools, and have no problem with spending half the year doing other things. But for poor students who have neither the time nor the money to indulge in such things, they are a disaster. The college year is even shorter than the high school year, and equally irrational. If liberal arts, that shibboleth of American education, is pushed down to the high school level, which is where it is in England, then colleges could focus on educating their students in specific disciplines. The current four year degree could be easily reduced to a two year degree, with no loss of content, and much greater mastery. Once again, there is nothing magical about four years, or three years. The issue is, what does it take to bring the student to the necessary level of understanding and knowledge in the specific discipline? Many students in America are currently taking longer than four years to complete their degrees (at their expense of course and to the financial benefit of the college) and this is ridiculous.

My son is currently a student at the University of Alabama, which has about 30,000 students, and offers degrees in everything imaginable. As is the norm in America there does not seem to be a course of study, but instead my son takes a number of courses, about 4 or five a semester, each worth 3 credits. Graduation requires 120 credits or 40 courses. Why a degree should require 120 credits as opposed to say 90 no one can explain. Because he is studying history (despite the fact that I tried to encourage him not to) he will end up with a debatable qualification (an undergraduate degree in history is not very marketable) or a need to go on to graduate school. Either way the university is smiling on their way to the bank.

Online education should be encouraged at all levels, provided always of course that it meets rigorous standards. For many students it is a much more cost effective way of achieving a degree. Universities and colleges tend to sneer at on-line education of course but unless they can demonstrate that it is inferior to their offerings, it is difficult to have much sympathy for their sneers. The brightest woman I know never went to college because in the era when she was born only boys went to college. After marriage and raising a large family she decided to do what she has always wanted to do – get a degree. At age 70 she enrolled in England's Open University, and duly obtained one, at very low cost, and with a great deal of pleasure.

Research

Education is something of a mess partly because, as we have seen, there is so little significant research about what works. That needs to change. If we do away with Colleges of Education as teacher prep programs, then perhaps they could do serious research on serious issues.

Research in how the brain works may have a significant impact, for instance. There is an approach called 'spaced learning'. In this approach, based on neurological research, short sharp lessons are interspersed with entirely different activities, and repeated at various intervals. For instance a child may be shown an eight minute powerpoint presentation, then play basketball, then repeat the powerpoint, and so on. There is no need for books, or paper, or pencils. Research has shown that connections between developing brain cells form most effectively when the brain is given regular breaks. The method shows that children can learn much more quickly and retain much more information through this process than by reading the traditional text book.

It is probable that most research will take place outside Colleges of Education. At one of the Universities to which my daughter is applying, Psychology is listed within the College of Education. Perhaps it would make more sense if the College were re-labeled the College of Applied Neuroscience.

Endword

Changing education is a herculean task, which is why all attempts up to now to educate all children have failed. Education is an enormous enterprise, and like all such entities, is very resistant to change. For there to be significant change educators need first to admit that there is failure, and this they are loath to do. There is a lot of talk and a lot of meetings, but few actions which make any difference. All Presidents and Prime Ministers and their staff talk about the value of education, but the more they talk the worse things seem to get.

If the culture of education is resistant to change, so too is the culture of poverty. If students are to benefit from schooling then their culture needs to embrace deferred gratification. Governments have a difficult enough time changing schools, which theoretically at least they control: how much more difficult is it to change the attitudes and values of students and their families, which are largely outside their control.

Not only does the structure and process of education need to change, therefore, but so does the culture of the people education serves. I think that this is beyond the present competence of governments in both America and England. But I hope I am wrong!

Selected References

Bloom, Allan, The Closing of the American Mind, Simon & Schuster, 1987

Bronfenbrenner, Urie: What Do Families Do? Family Affairs, Winter/Spring 1991, Vol 4, No1-2.

Gardner, Howard, The Unschooled Mind, Basic Books, 1991

Harris, Judith Rich, The Nurture Assumption, The Free Press, 1998

Healy, Jane M., Endangered Minds, Simon & Schuster, 1990

Herrnstein, Richard J, and Charles Murray, The Bell Curve, The Free Press, 1994

Jensen, Arthur R, Genetics and Education, Harper and Row, 1972

Kozol, Jonathan, Illiterate America, New American Library, 1985

Nisbett, Richard E, Intelligence and How to Get It, W W Norton and Company, 2009

Pinker, Steven, The Black Slate, Viking, 2002

Ravitch, Diane, Left Back. Simon & Schuster, 2000

Ridley, Matt, Nature Via Nurture, Harper Collins, 2003

Sachs, Jeffrey D, The End of Poverty, Penguin Books, 2006

Wilson, William Julius, The Truly Disadvantaged, The University of Chicago Press, 1987.